SIMPLE BEGINNINGS:
Soldering Jewelry

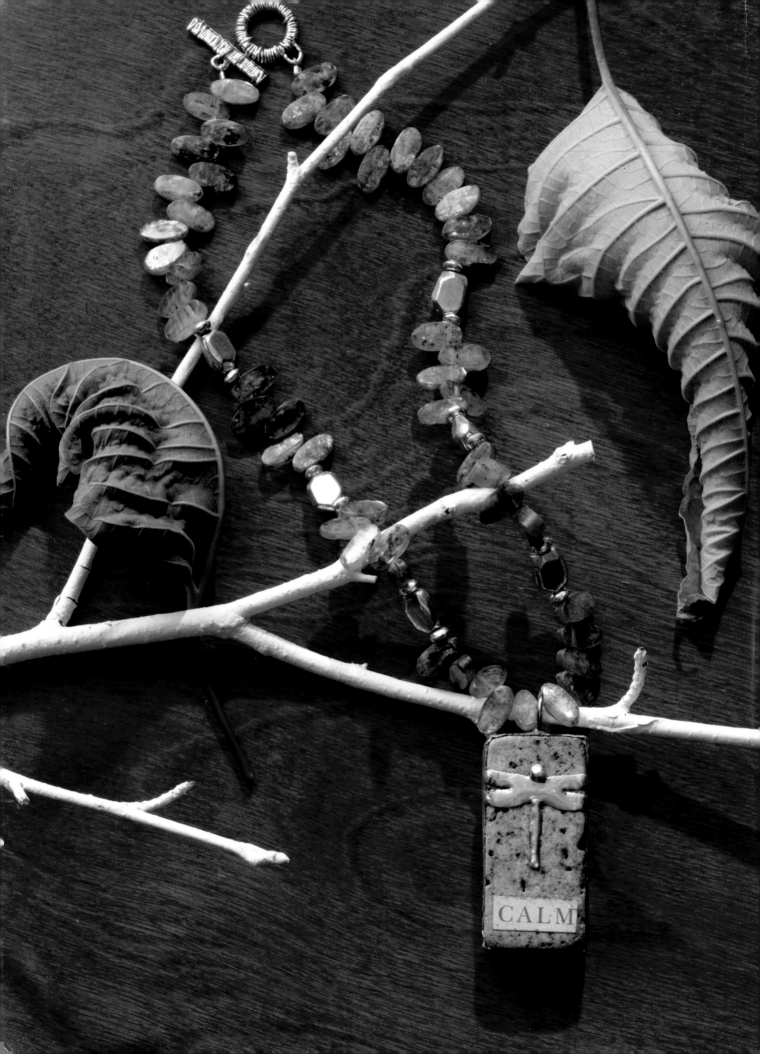

SIMPLE BEGINNINGS:
Soldering Jewelry

A Step-by-Step Guide to Creating Your Own Necklaces, Bracelets, Rings & More

Suzann Sladcik Wilson

Design Originals

an Imprint of Fox Chapel Publishing

www.d-originals.com

Calming Waters, page 74.

Dedication:

This book is dedicated to my husband Kevin and my son Craig. Thank you for being my biggest cheerleaders. I love you both!

—Suzann

Special thanks to the following people for their assistance in
the writing of this book:

William K. Sladcik, James Wheeler, Lucy Conception, and Damien Thompson of Sladcik Wheeler Photography. Thank you for always making me, and my jewelry, look so good!

To Susan Nattoli Wade of The Artisan's Workshop—your ability to teach is an amazing gift! Thank you for sharing your talents and for inspiring this book.

Karen Lange Doyle and Celene Persaud Morales—your love, support, and laughter are what helped me make it through during the writing of this book. You gals rock!

Peg Couch—it was a soldered pendant that started it all! Thank you for believing in me and for making my dreams come true.

Katie Weeber—no one could ask for a better editor! Thank you for your guidance through this process. You have the patience of a saint and a heart of gold.

Photography by William K. Sladcik and Suzann Sladcik Wilson.

Hand model: Angelina Pizzi.

Special thanks to Euro Tool, Inc. for the use of the photos appearing on pages 16, 17, 18, and 21.

ISBN 978-1-57421-416-1

Library of Congress Cataloging-in-Publication Data

Wilson, Suzann Sladcik.
 Simple beginnings : soldering jewelry / Suzann Sladcik Wilson.
    pages cm
 Includes index.
 Summary: "Soldering is a popular jewelry-making technique that can produce beautiful results, but if you've never had the chance to pick up a soldering iron, the process can seem daunting. Where can you find the tools you will need? What do you do with them once you have them? And what materials should you work with? In Simple Beginnings: Soldering Jewelry, renowned artist Suzann Sladcik Wilson will put all these questions to rest. Wilson will take you to the very beginning of the soldering process and teach you about the tools you will need and the materials you should buy. Then, she will take you step-by-step through the basic soldering techniques you will need to know to create your own woks of art using copper foil. Projects for beginner, intermediate, and advanced craft enthusiasts are included, ensuring that you'll always have something new to inspire and create as your skills increase. Use this book to make pendants, bracelets, earrings, frames, and more, all in your own unique, creative style. Get started today!"-- Provided by publisher.

 ISBN 978-1-57421-416-1 (pbk.)
 1. Jewelry making. 2. Solder and soldering. I. Title.
 TT212.W565 2012
 745.594'2--dc23

                2012016216

Printed in China

First Printing

About the Author

Author Suzann Sladcik Wilson.
Photo by Alysa Correll
Clark of Water Street
Dreams.

Joy is the theme that runs through all of Suzann Sladcik Wilson's work. Whether she is designing an original piece of jewelry for a client, introducing a student to the joy of beading and jewelry design, or hosting or appearing as a guest on radio shows, her message is about empowerment through creativity and inspiration.

For more than eighteen years, Wilson has been and continues to be a master in her field. Using only the highest quality materials of Swarovski crystals, Hill Tribe silver, artisan beads, and more, Wilson creates beauty and joy in the form of earrings, necklaces, bracelets, and watches, and instructs her followers to do the same. In a time when many individuals are searching for something more, Wilson teaches all of her students how to maximize their minds, bodies, and spirits by using the power of jewelry design, coupled with the drive of their passions, to create and inspire.

As an artist, author, educator, consultant, entrepreneur, and philanthropist, Wilson is as successful as she is busy. Her blogs, articles, and jewelry designs have appeared all over the web and in print. In her professional jewelry design career, Wilson has been published in *Bead Style, Simply Beads Magazine, Bead Trends,* on the website *epatterns.com,* and in the books *Four Seasons of Beading* and *Earrings, Earrings, Earrings!.* In 2012, she published her first book, *Simple Beginnings: Beading,* with Fox Chapel Publishing.

Wilson has been a guest on *Military Mom Radio* and *Motherhood Talk Radio,* each show reaching 60,000 listeners. Additionally, Wilson has been a substitute host on the Her Insight Radio Network. She is also a Professional Designer Member of the Craft and Hobby Association, where she serves on the Designer Trends Panel, reporting on the bead and jewelry-making industries. In January 2011, she received the coveted Craft and Hobby Association Designer Press Kit award for an innovative necklace design. An active contributor and participant in many charities, Wilson strives to make the world a better place for today's and our future's children.

Suzann Sladcik Wilson was born in Chicago, Illinois. She attended Loyola University of Chicago, earning her Bachelor's Degree in Education. She continues to expand her professional knowledge of beading and jewelry making by attending the yearly Bead and Button Show in Milwaukee, Wisconsin, subscribing and contributing to several leading beading and jewelry-making magazines, and networking with several other leading designers.

Wilson currently splits her time between Chicago, Illinois, Door County, Wisconsin, and occasionally Frankfurt, Germany. You can learn more by visiting Suzann online at *http://beadphoria.wordpress.com* or *www.beadphoriaboutique.com*.

Contents

Pendants
62

Feeling Green, 62

Flights of Memory, 63

Shine On!, 64

treasure

Passion, 66

Sizzlin' Hot, 67

World Traveler, 68

Treasure , 65

Necklaces
69

Ancient Glass, 69

Siren's Song, 70

Flower Power, 71

Vintage Photography, 72

Fresh Picked, 73

Calming Waters, 74

Bracelets
75

Steampunk Time, 75

Ants Go Marching, 76

Heart on My Sleeve, 77

Other Jewelry
78

Royal Rings, 78

Filled With Hope
Awareness Pin, 79

Fancy Face Floral Pin, 80

Halloween Treat, 81

Golden Glam Earrings, 82

Discover all you need to know about soldering!

Pre-soldering supplies, page 25.

Soldering tools, page 15,

Soldering iron tips, page 15.

Using broken or shattered materials, page 26.

Stamping on glass and other materials, page 28.

Jewelry findings, page 32.

Altering glass, page 46.

Incorporating images into projects, page 64.

Coloring solder, page 50.

Creative projects, page 60.

Inspirational ideas, page 84.

Step-by-step tutorials, page 42.

Introduction:
Create Without Fear!

If you walk into a chic boutique today, you will likely find a display featuring beautiful necklaces with pendants that contain miniature works of art enclosed in glass and edged with a glimmering silver frame. You might pause to admire the jewelry, thinking, "These must take a lot of time to craft, and they're probably difficult to make!" If you think making soldered jewelry is a lengthy and challenging process, I have good news to share with you! Making basic soldered jewelry pieces is fast and easy, while enabling you to take your jewelry designs to a whole new level.

If you are like me, the idea of using a soldering torch to melt metal with an open flame can be scary. But this is not the only way to work with metal. In fact, you can melt metal in a controlled way without an open flame by using a soldering iron. Fear of using a hot object like a soldering iron might make you hesitate and prevent you from exploring your creativity to make your own custom soldered jewelry components. Don't be afraid! If you have twirled a curling iron, worked with a glue gun, or passed over paper with an embossing tool, you already have the knowledge you need to handle a soldering iron.

In this book, I am here to help guide you on your journey through the wonderful world of soldering. You will learn about the tools and supplies you need, the variety of materials you can work with, and how to make your own miniature works of art. You will find simple step-by-step instructions to walk you through your first soldering project and a jewelry designs chapter you can use to practice your new artistry once you've mastered the basic skills. Finally, when you are ready to develop your own soldering designs, turn to the inspirational ideas chapter.

Soldering allows you to express yourself by making distinctive jewelry pieces that you will enjoy for years to come. I look forward to walking with you as you discover the creativity and fun soldering has to offer. Let's get started!

—Suzann Sladcik Wilson

1

Tools

Soldering tools do not take up a large amount of space, which is a perfect reason to try your hand at making soldered jewelry. In addition, you won't have to purchase expensive equipment before you can start creating. Everything you need will easily fit on the surface of a round kitchen table and can be purchased at local craft stores without breaking your budget. Soldering tools are easy to set up and just as easy to pack away and store when you are finished. Once you understand the basics of the necessary tools, you will be stocking a soldering studio of your own!

Pre-Soldering Tools

Look around your home and you will be able to find most of the tools needed to assemble the pendants and other jewelry components you will go on to solder. If you are missing any items, a quick trip to your local craft store will be all you need to complete your project toolbox. You will note that a few of these items are repeated in the Soldering Tools section. You can use some of the same tools for assembling your jewelry components and soldering them; you will just use them for different tasks.

Craft scissors

Craft scissors: A sharp pair of small crafting scissors will make it easy for you to cut out and trim the items you want to include in your jewelry components.

Paintbrushes: Keep a variety of paintbrushes on hand. Foam brushes work well for spreading decoupage glue over large areas. Smaller brushes will be a benefit when placing glue, ink, or paint on small pieces. Designate one brush for the different mediums you use, like glue, paint, and glitter. This will keep your glue the proper color and glitter out of your paint!

Suzann's Sensational Soldering Tip

Be edgy! Edging scissors with decorative blades, typically used for scrapbooking and paper crafts, are a great way to give your paper and copper foil a whole new look!

Tweezers: The projects you will make to be encased in glass and soldered are truly miniature works of art with minute pieces and elements. Tweezers make it easy to pick up small pieces of paper and other items and place them exactly where you want.

Shaped paper punches: Visit the scrapbooking section of your local craft store to find shaped paper punches. These allow you to cut perfectly formed tiny shapes out of any type of paper.

Paintbrushes

Soldering Tools

You might already have a basic jewelry-making tool kit for beading or other jewelry-making projects, but to branch out into soldering, you will need a specific set of tools to make your miniature works of art. The following presents all the tools you should have on hand to successfully fashion your own soldered jewelry.

Suzann's Sensational Soldering Tip

Pick the right tip. You will need to replace the tip of your soldering iron periodically, depending how often you use it. When selecting a replacement, make sure you purchase one made by the manufacturer that produced your soldering iron. Soldering iron tips are often specific to a particular brand of iron and, sometimes, even a particular model.

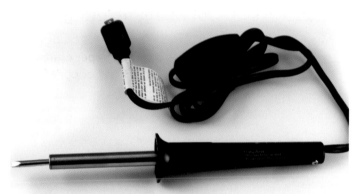

Soldering iron

Soldering iron: Your soldering iron is similar to a paintbrush. There is a large variety on the market, so make sure you choose the one that is right for what you want to do. Soldering Irons are sold according to wattage, or in other words, the amount of heat they produce. Make sure you select a soldering iron that produces *at least* sixty to one hundred watts. This ensures your soldering iron will get hot enough to melt lead-free solder. Also, purchase a soldering iron that has a *chisel-shaped tip*. With its flat surface, a chisel-shaped tip makes covering your copper foil easy.

Soldering iron stand: While it is turned on, your soldering iron is extremely hot! A stand will keep your work surface from being burned and prevent your iron from rolling off the edge of your work area.

Soldering Iron Tips

❑ Regularly check your iron's cord for burns or cracks. Have a professional replace the cord if necessary, or replace the iron altogether.

❑ Store your soldering iron only after it has cooled for several hours. Then, seal it in a plastic bag to prevent corrosion caused by humidity.

❑ Be attentive to the temperature of your soldering iron. If it's too cool, it will not melt the solder as needed. If it's too hot, it can melt the adhesive on the back of your copper foil tape, creating a sticky residue. An extremely hot iron can also crack the glass of your project.

Soldering iron stand

Beading tweezers: Think of your tweezers as an extension of your hand that you use when applying solder to your new creations. During soldering, the heat of the soldering iron you are using will make the project you are working on extremely hot. With their long jaws, beading tweezers are a great tool that will allow you to safely hold and move your piece while soldering. Always use tweezers during the time you are working with a soldering iron to change the position of your project to avoid burning your fingertips!

Bone folder: Typically used in paper crafting to create sharp creases, a bone folder is the perfect tool to make sure the copper foil tape sticks properly to the edges of your project. By using the bone folder to properly burnish (rub) the copper foil over your glass, you will ensure that flux or cleaner will not seep under the copper foil tape and ruin your piece. When burnishing with your bone folder, make sure you apply firm, even pressure, but don't use so much pressure that you risk cracking the glass or other elements of your project.

File: Occasionally, your finished soldered piece will have a bump or burr in the metal. A file or emery board will help remove these small blemishes. Files can also be used to bring finished pieces to a glamorous high shine.

Flux brush: When working with a chemical like flux, it is best to reserve a brush that you only use with that chemical. Flux brushes typically have silver handles with black bristles. They are very inexpensive, so you might want to keep several on hand near your workstation.

Bead tweezers

Bone folder

Suzann's Sensational Soldering Tip
Rub a file across paper or other similar objects to give them an aged, distressed look, or give glass a cloudy or frosty look by running a file over the surface.

Flux brush. Photo courtesy of Euro Tool, Inc.

Heat-resistant ceramic tile

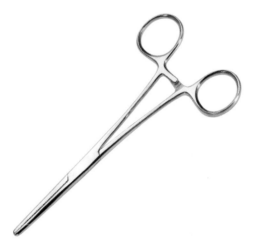

Hemostat. Photo courtesy of Euro Tool, Inc.

Heat-resistant surface: You want to work on a surface that will not be damaged by the high heat of your soldering iron or metal solder. A large ceramic tile from your local home improvement store will do the trick. In addition to being heat resistant, the tile wipes clean quickly and easily.

Hemostats: Although normally found in a hospital or your doctor's office, hemostats are perfect for soldering, giving you surgical precision when making your jewelry. A hemostat looks like a pair of scissors with small, ridged jaws at the tip rather than blades. It contains a mechanism in the handle that allows you to lock the tip closed. Using this locking mechanism, you can grip a jump ring securely with the hemostat, enabling you to easily attach it to your soldered piece with complete accuracy. I usually keep several on hand in my soldering studio. You can find hemostats at flea markets, medical supply shops, or through online retailers.

Nonstick scissors: You will need scissors to cut copper foil tape and trim the edges of your project when necessary. Scissors with nonstick blades are perfect for cutting copper foil tape.

Rheostat: When it comes to melting your solder, the correct temperature is key. A rheostat lets you control the temperature of your soldering iron. A rheostat contains a dial similar to those on your stove. The higher you turn the dial, the more heat is released from the device. Rheostats can be found as individual units, but I prefer to work with those that are part of a soldering station. The soldering station helps me keep my supplies organized, close at hand, and safe.

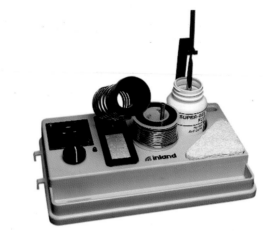

Rheostat

Synthetic sponge: For periodically cleaning the tip of your soldering iron, keep a moistened synthetic sponge on hand. Avoid sponges made of natural materials, because they have a much lower burn point than synthetic sponges.

Third hand: Couldn't we all use a third hand? In this instance, a third hand made for soldering saves the day and your fingers! This tool holds your jewelry in place so you can add a jump ring. I prefer working with a third hand rather than clamps, finding it much more stable and unlikely to tip over.

Synthetic sponge

Third hand. Photo courtesy of Euro Tool, Inc.

Jewelry-Making Tools

After you finish making your glamorous soldered pieces, you will definitely want to show off by displaying them on a piece of jewelry. Keep these jewelry-making tools on hand, and you will be able create dazzling jewelry that will make your soldered creations shine!

Pliers

Every beader should work with a reliable set of pliers. Pliers allow you to bend wire, make loops, get into hard-to-reach places, and add crimp tubes to a jewelry design. You can often find pliers designed specifically for beading as a set.

Bent-nose pliers

Bent-nose pliers: The jaws of bent-nose pliers are easy to identify, because they are tapered like regular jewelry-making pliers, but are then bent at an angle near the tip. These are the pliers to turn to when you need to get into tight spaces.

Chain-nose pliers: Chain-nose pliers, also known as needle-nose pliers, have a smooth flat surface on the interior of the jaws. The small tapered point allows you to get into small areas. You will typically use this tool for gripping jewelry findings and working with wire.

Chain-nose pliers

Crimping pliers: Crimping pliers are one of the cornerstone tools of beading and were designed specifically for jewelry making. Their purpose is to flatten and bend a small tube of metal, called a crimp tube or crimp, to securely finish a necklace or bracelet so your jewelry will stay together for years to come. When purchasing crimping pliers, make sure you buy regular-sized ones, not micro or mighty crimping pliers. Regular crimping pliers are meant for 2 x 2mm crimp tubes, which are what you will use when making most of your jewelry.

Crimping pliers

Flat-nose pliers: With large flat rectangular jaws, flat-nose pliers are useful for holding and bending wire. Flat-nose pliers give you the ability to grip objects tightly, because of their large surface area.

Round-nose pliers: The jaws of round-nose pliers are, of course, round, and taper to a point at each tip. The cone-like shape of each jaw enables you to make different-sized loops for earrings, pendants, and wirework. Round-nose pliers can also be utilized to help grip small areas.

Other essentials

Don't forget these next few tools. They're also necessary items you will need in your jewelry-making toolbox.

Bead board: A bead board is to a jewelry maker what canvas is to a painter. Bead boards give you a place to lay your radiant beads out before stringing, so you can have a preview of your finished piece. There are many types of bead boards available. Most are gray and have one or more shallow channels. The best boards for beginners are flocked (covered in minute fiber particles) so your beads have a non-slip surface. I suggest beginning jewelry makers purchase a necklace bead board with three channels, rather than just one. Not long after you start making jewelry, you will want to try making multi-strand necklaces, and with a three-channel board, you are equipped to do so. A bead board's outer channel is measured in inches, while the innermost channel is measured in centimeters.

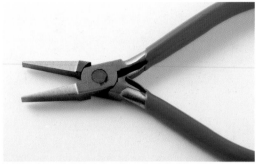

Flat-nose pliers

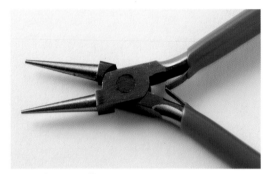

Round-nose pliers

Suzann's Sensational Soldering Tip

If you find a place on the jaws of your round-nose pliers that makes a perfect-sized loop, take a permanent marker and mark the spot. By consistently using the same place on your pliers, you will always make loops of the same size.

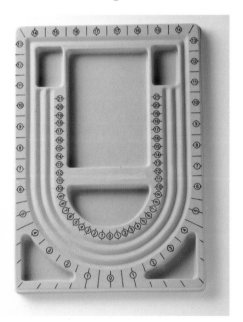

Bead board

Bead mat. Photo courtesy of Euro Tool, Inc.

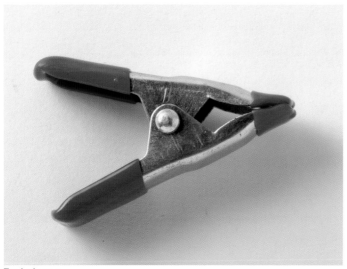

End clamp

Wire cutters

Bead mat: These practical mats are soft, fuzzy, and will save you lots of frustration. Their wooly material keeps beads from rolling away from your jewelry-making area. Bead mats often come in many different colors. They are very inexpensive, so it is worth having a few on hand.

End clamps: There is nothing more heartbreaking than picking up your beautiful necklace design after you have strung your all your beads and watching them fall off the other end. Over the years, I have tried many different methods of keeping my designs intact when moving them. The best solution I've discovered is the end clamp. End clamps are about 2" (51mm) long and have rubber tips. The rubber keeps the clamp in place without kinking your wire. Most beaders I know keep several in their toolbox to use on pieces in progress.

Wire cutters: Wire cutters are the workhorse of your toolbox. You will use your wire cutters on everything from beading wire to head pins and eye pins. I recommend using flush cutters to obtain the straightest cuts. If your wire cutters are leaving burrs (jagged edges) or you need to use excessive force to complete a cut, the blades might be worn down and you may want to replace your cutters.

2

Materials and Supplies

The number of materials and supplies you can use to create a soldered piece of jewelry is staggering. There is endless opportunity for originality, ingenuity, and innovation. And just like the tools used for soldering, you don't have to empty out your wallet to get great materials. You can use store-bought patterned paper, or you can clip colored designs from a magazine. You can purchase   pieces of fabric or cut a piece of cloth from a favorite T-shirt that can't be worn anymore. You closet, your kitchen, and your garden are all places you should examine for useful soldered jewelry materials. And don't forget to check out your local craft store for colorful stickers or beading supplies.

There is no limit to the supplies and materials you can incorporate into a soldered project. Visit your local craft store to get an idea of what's available. And don't forget to look in your own home, too. Some of the best projects you make will contain personal items that have sentimental value to you.

Finding Materials and Supplies

If you've never been shopping for soldering, paper, or jewelry-making supplies, the number of resources available might take you by surprise. You will of course be able to locate most of what you need at your local craft store, but you should also check out some of the other places listed below to locate some unique, one-of-a-kind elements.

Bead shows: Bead shows are dizzying places with mountains of glimmering beads and piles of shinny jewelry findings. Most items are sold in bulk, so if you want to create a large number of pieces, you may want to check out a local bead show so you can get everything you need from one place.

Craft superstores: Today's craft superstores have an amazing array of products. Here, you should be able to find everything from beautiful beads and gorgeous glass to a plethora of paper. Some craft superstores also have stained glass departments that carry everything you need to get started with soldering. If you are looking for one particular item, call ahead to see if your local store carries the specific item you need.

Hardware and home improvement stores: You might be surprised by the amount of materials and supplies hardware stores can offer those interested in soldering. Soldering irons, copper foil tape, lead-free solder, ceramic tiles, and glass can often be located here. Don't forget to check the paint department and small hardware section to purchase some extra supplies to add special touches to your projects.

Independent bead, stained glass, and scrapbook stores: Your local independent bead, scrapbook, and stained glass stores can be very encouraging places to shop for materials and supplies. The staff is usually well educated and willing to help answer any questions you may have.

Internet sites: Some of the tools and supplies listed in this book may be challenging to locate in your area. Turn to your computer and let it save the day!

Specialty stores, garage sales, and flea markets: Looking for something distinctive for your project? Antique, resale, and thrift stores, garage sales, and flea markets are sensational places to find ephemera, beads, glass, and other useful objects. Sometimes, if you are lucky, you can even pick up soldering supplies like hemostats and tweezers. One of the advantages of shopping at these locations is you can pick up a wide variety of items for an extremely low price.

Suzann's Sensational Soldering Tip

Get cutting! You might need to cut a piece of glass to a certain size for some of your projects. When this is the case, I prefer to leave the cutting to the professionals rather than run the risk of injuring myself. Stores that offer picture framing can often do the job for little to no money. Stained glass and many hardware stores also have the ability to cut glass on demand.

Pre-Soldering Supplies

There is no set list of supplies you need to assemble a pendant or other jewelry component. You can use just about any material you want. Searching for supplies can take you on a wonderful tour around your local craft store. Explore areas like the scrapbook section, floral aisle, and paint section to be inspired. You'll also want to examine the contents of your keepsake box or even your jeans pocket to see if you have a piece of ephemera lurking there. The following list is just the beginning of what you can use to create soldered jewelry. Get creative and add to the list as you come across additional items you want to use.

Pre-packaged glass: Microscope slides, memory glass slides, and glass shapes cut specifically for copper foil soldering come pre-packaged for the general crafter.

Stained glass shapes: The technique used in this book was derived from methods developed by stained glass artisans. Stained glass suppliers carry a wide array of glass in different shapes, sizes, and colors. Many stores will even cut the glass for you if you are looking for a specialty size or shape.

Glass 'stones': Often used as fillers for vases and table decorations, glass stones with flat bottoms can be turned into stunning pendants using the copper foil soldering technique. These stones come in a wide range of colors, so let your imagination go wild when developing designs to incorporate them.

Mosaic pieces: Making mosaic pieces, especially stepping stones for the garden, has become more popular in recent years. Because of this, you will find a variety of glass and ceramic mosaic components in different shapes and sizes. Pre-packaged and available in most craft and hobby stores, you can easily find mosaic pieces that are simple to solder and can quickly be made into jewelry pieces.

Suzann's Sensational Soldering Tip

Today, there is no reason to learn how to cut your own glass. Buying glass that has already been cut or formed saves you the time and hassle of trying to cut your own. Microscope slides, pre-made glass shapes in the scrapbook section, and pieces for stained glass projects are easy to find and are perfect for copper foil soldered projects.

Pre-packaged glass pieces

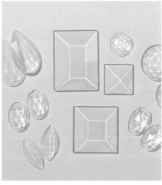

Stained glass shapes

Mosaic pieces

Sea glass: Walking along the beach, you might come across sea or beach glass. These are pieces of broken glass that have been smoothed by the waves and etched by the sand, removing most of the jagged edges and producing a frosted appearance. This glass can add a unique touch to a soldered piece.

Broken bits: Accidentally shattering a plate or piece of pottery that has sentimental value can be heartbreaking. But don't be too disheartened—you can salvage those broken pieces and incorporate them into your jewelry designs! That way, you are able to keep a token of your plate or pottery, and people will still get to admire it as a part of your jewelry piece.

Other 'solderable' objects: You can find many other items besides glass that are perfect for a soldered piece. Stones, tiles, coins, game pieces, and even bottle caps can be transformed into jewelry pieces that will have your designs turning heads.

Sea glass

Suzann's Sensational Soldering Tip

Smooth the rough edges. If you are working with broken pieces of glass or pottery, you may want to file down any sharp edges. This will keep your copper foil (and your fingers!) intact when you are wrapping the piece.

Broken bits

Other "solderable" objects

Suzann's Sensational Soldering Tip

Keep in mind the thickness of your piece while you are designing it. If the jewelry component becomes too bulky, the copper foil will not be able to wrap around the edges and you won't be able to apply solder.

Suzann's Sensational Soldering Tip

Print with caution! If you are printing digital images, whether your own photos or clip art, use matte or semi-matte paper. Glossy paper has a tendency to stick to glass and cause the image to look distorted or "wet" when heated.

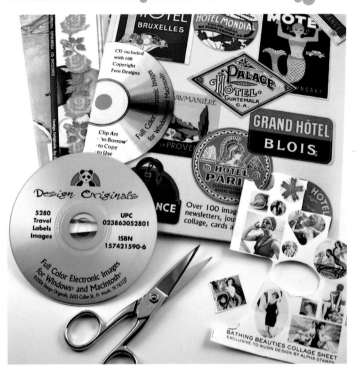

Clip art

Ephemera

Clip art: If you're searching for images for your jewelry components, clip art can be a fantastic resource. Traditionally clip art is found in clip art books, but with today's technology, you can easily purchase clip art to download from the Internet.

Decoupage glue: Your jewelry components will be framed in glass, so it is important to create them using glue that dries clear. Consider using decoupage glue with a matte finish when creating your jewelry components.

Decoupage glue

Ephemera: As we travel through life, we often accumulate bits of paper like labels, movie tickets, playbills, and other similar objects that may or may not have sentimental meaning to us. These remnants can be just what you are looking for when it comes to completing a jewelry design. Concert tickets, snippets of fabric, and old trading cards are just a few examples of ephemera that can make your project design truly unique!

Markers: Regular markers, permanent markers, and paint markers are all brilliant ways to bring color to your designs. Use regular markers to color stamps and then stamp the paper you plan to incorporate in your jewelry component. Permanent markers and paint pens can be used on nonporous surfaces like metal, glass, or stone to give a punch of color in unexpected places.

Paper

Photos

Paper: Think of paper as the canvas for your projects. Scrapbook paper, wrapping paper, and artisan paper all make excellent choices for soldered jewelry components.

Photos: Photos of meaningful people and places can turn a soldered pendant into a cherished keepsake. Any new mother or grandmother would love to receive a pendant with the picture of a new little one in it.

Stickers and transfers: Stickers and transfers typically used by scrapbook artists can help you quickly create your miniature works of art. With thousands of choices, you are sure to find stickers and transfers that express your passion. Use them to create any look you desire— vintage, modern, whimsical, or anything else.

Stamps and inks: Stamps and inks can bring a whole new dimension to various elements of your project. You can use them on paper as is traditional, or go a step further and try them on glass, stones, and metal by applying ink designed for non-porous surfaces.

Suzann's Sensational Soldering Tip

Make memories. Looking for ways to preserve your family memories without destroying the original photograph? A scanner connected to your computer can be a very useful tool.

Stickers and transfers

Stamps and inks

SIMPLE BEGINNINGS: Soldering Jewelry

Soldering Supplies

Just like you need specific soldering tools to create soldered jewelry, you also need a handful of soldering supplies. The following is everything you need to get started on your first project.

Copper foil tape: Copper foil tape comes in a variety of widths. Tape ¼" (6mm) or ⅝" (16mm) wide is most commonly used for copper foil soldering. Purchase tape with a black backing; tape with a copper backing can show as a shiny reflection through the glass of a pendant or other jewelry component. Large copper foil sheets with adhesive backs are available for use on projects with a large surface area. These sheets are also useful if you want to cut out a specialty shape for a project.

Flux: Although flux is a chemical, it often helps to think of it as glue—it holds the solder to the copper foil tape. Without it, the solder will not stick to the copper foil. There are three types of flux available on the market: liquid, gel, and paste. Liquid flux is widely used but can evaporate quickly, produce fumes, and smoke. I prefer gel flux. It is often water soluble for easy clean up and doesn't evaporate as quickly as the liquid version. Gel flux doesn't smoke like liquid flux and is typically odorless and free of fumes. Paste flux is not recommended for this technique. Flux remover is available for those times when an amount of flux remains on a project after soldering.

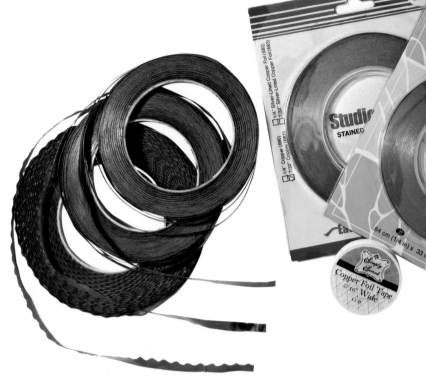

Copper foil tape

Flux

Glass or multi-purpose cleaner: When you've finished a piece, you want it to look it's best. Use glass or a multi-purpose cleaner to remove flux or fingerprints from the project. A multi-purpose cleaner that cleans both glass and metal is a great choice, as it cleans the glass and polishes the metal solder at the same time!

Jump rings: Attach these metal rings to a soldered piece so it can be hung from a necklace, connected to other soldered pieces to make a bracelet, or to create a bead dangle for the bottom of a pin. Use 16- or 18-gauge jump rings, as they will be able to stand up to the wear and tear put on them as part of a piece of jewelry.

Lead-free solder: Because your soldered items will most likely be worn against the skin, it is *extremely important* that you use lead-free solder. Using lead-free solder also ensures that you will not inhale potentially harmful fumes while soldering. Solder is most often sold in single pound (450 gram) spools, with smaller sizes sometimes available. A pound of solder will last you a very long time, as each project only requires a small amount.

Suzann's Sensational Soldering Tip

Stick with sterling. Sterling silver jump rings, while a little more expensive than base metal jump rings, seem to be easier to attach to solder and match the color of lead-free solder well.

Lead-free solder

Jewelry-Making Supplies

When you are finished soldering your jewelry component, you will want a way to highlight your glamorous new piece of jewelry. By keeping a few essential jewelry-making supplies and materials on hand in your soldering studio, you will have everything you need to make pins with passion, beautiful bracelets, stylish necklaces, and more.

Beads

Beads come in all sorts of shapes, sizes, colors, and materials. Taking a little extra consideration when choosing your beads will give you a marvelous finished jewelry piece that will call attention to your amazing new soldering talents. Keep in mind the following when acquiring your beads:

Color: Beads come in every hue you can dream of. Pick colors that will complement and draw out the colors contained in your soldered piece, or for an added element of drama, select beads in colors that contrast the shades in your miniature work of art. Bring your soldered piece with you when shopping for beads to ensure you get the correct tones.

Size: Bead sizes range from tiny seed beads that are no larger than a period to oversized chunky beads that can be as big as a golf ball! To determine the size you need, consider the shape of your soldered piece and the size of the opening of the attached jump ring. If the beads are too small, the jump ring on a soldered pendant might slide over them and out of its intended place while the piece is being worn. Beads that are too big can overwhelm a soldered piece and draw attention away from your fabulous work.

Style: Your finished soldered piece will have a distinct style, and by incorporating it into a piece of jewelry, it's like you are telling a small story. You want the story behind your soldered work to match the story expressed by the beads you select. The style of beads can help translate what you want to say. Pearls and crystals can give a jewelry piece a romantic look, while wooden and organic beads provide a more natural feel. Using metal and stone can create an edgy piece.

Other jewelry-making supplies

Beads are certainly an important part of the jewelry-making supplies you'll need to present your finished soldered pieces, but beads on their own can't form a necklace! Here are some additional jewelry-making essentials you'll want to have on hand.

Beading wire: Flexible beading wire really is the backbone of your jewelry designs. You will use it to string your beads and soldered pieces for the vast majority of your necklace and bracelet creations. Flexible beading wire is made of strands of steel woven together and covered with a nylon coating. You can find it woven in 7-, 19-, 21-, or 49-strand counts. The higher the strand count, the more flexible the wire and the more expensive it is. Flexible beading wire comes in a variety of thicknesses. Fine wire (0.010" or 0.25mm in diameter) works well with pearls and other beads with small holes, while thicker wire (0.024" or 0.61mm) can be used for heavy beads. I prefer to use Soft Flex brand's medium 0.019" (0.48mm)/21-strand wire in original satin silver. The wire has a medium thickness and will fit through the holes in almost all of your beads. Its flexibility also allows the jewelry to lie beautifully. Select a brand of beading wire that works with your soldered piece and the beads you've selected. While shopping for wire, you may see that some brands of beading wire are labeled "Good," "Better," and "Best." This is just another way of describing the thread count of the wire.

Barrel clasp: A barrel clasp has two pieces that are screwed together to make a closure. These were once a popular alternative for lobster claw clasps. Unfortunately, barrel clasps have a tendency to become undone on their own and should be used with caution.

Flexible beading wire

Barrel clasps

Box or tab clasp: Some of the most adorned and elaborate clasps are box or tab clasps. This closure is made by inserting a tab into a box-like shape. Some box clasps include a safety mechanism that prevents the tab from accidentally coming out.

Box clasp

Crimp tubes: Crimp tubes, sometimes referred to as crimps, are small metal tubes with thin walls that are used on flexible beading wire to attach clasps and finish designs. When you go to purchase crimps, you will find both crimp tubes and crimp beads. I recommend using crimp tubes over crimp beads, because they give crimping pliers a large surface area to grip. Purchase a pack of 2 x 2mm crimp tubes that are either gold-filled or sterling silver. You might see crimp tubes available in base metal, but you will find sterling silver or gold-filled tubes crimp more easily and the results are more consistent. It is well worth it to pay a few extra pennies for quality crimp tubes that will keep your designs intact.

Folded crimps: Making jewelry with leather, cord, or ribbon can be fun, and folding crimp ends make attaching a clasp a breeze. A folding crimp has a loop at one end, enabling you to use a jump ring to attach a clasp or to crimp a section of stringing material to serve as a clasp loop. Add a dab of jewelry glue to the inside of a folding crimp to be sure your leather, cord, or ribbon stays in place.

Folded crimps

Crimp tubes

Hook and eye clasps

Lobster clasp

Magnetic clasps

Hook and eye clasp: One half of this clasp consists of one piece that looks like an oversized *J*, while the other half is a ring or loop. The *J* piece is hooked onto the ring to close the clasp. The best use of hook and eye clasps is in necklaces. There might not be enough tension in a bracelet to keep a hook and eye clasp closed.

Lobster claw clasp: These clasps are named for their close resemblance to a lobster claw. The "claw" mechanism is usually latched on to a jump ring, a link of chain, or another open loop to close a necklace or bracelet. These clasps are the most secure closures available, but because of their sturdy construction, the lever on the clasp can be difficult to open and close by the person wearing the jewelry.

Magnetic clasp: Using magnets to keep the two parts of the clasp together, a magnetic clasp is easy to open and close and comes in a wide variety of styles. The magnets can be demagnetized over time, however, causing your clasp to fall apart. Because the magnets are often tiny, these clasps should not be incorporated in jewelry for small children, because they are a choking hazard. Magnets can also affect electronic equipment, such as a pacemaker. Avoid giving jewelry with magnetic clasps to individuals with health problems who might be required to use a pacemaker or other similar equipment.

S-hook clasp: This clasp is similar to a hook and eye clasp, except one half is shaped like an *S* instead of a *J*. The clasp is closed by slipping one of the curves of the *S* through a jump ring, ring, or loop. S-hook clasps are best for necklaces, since the weight of the jewelry creates tension to keep the clasp closed. Many S-hook clasps are quite ornate. Consider using them as a decorative element when designing your jewelry.

S-hook clasps

Toggle clasp: Toggle clasps are one of the most popular and simplest closures for necklaces and bracelets. They consist of two pieces, a bar and a loop. The bar is put through the loop and laid flat to close a jewelry piece. When choosing a toggle, make sure the bar portion overlaps the loop far enough so the toggle will not slip apart.

Toggle clasp

Earring findings

A small soldered piece might be overlooked as a pendant on a necklace or bracelet design, but these small pieces are perfect for earrings. To make earrings, you'll need to have the following supplies.

Chandeliers

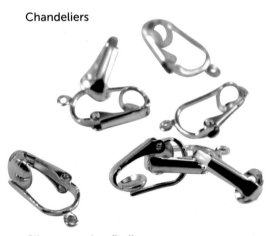

Clip-on earring findings

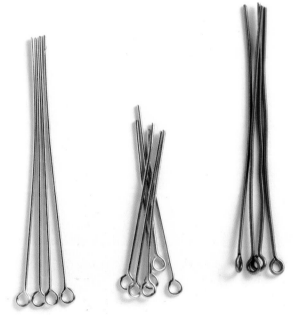

Eye pins

Chandeliers: Add an extra bit of elegance to your earrings by using chandeliers. These earring findings are used for dangling designs, letting beads and soldered components swing and move freely. They are perfect for individuals with long necks.

Clip-ons: These are not your grandmother's clip-ons. Today's designs are styled in such a way that they look like earrings created for pierced ears. Many clip-ons now come with adjustable tension, allowing the wearer to personalize the fit, keeping her ears from feeling pinched.

Eye pins: Eye pins look similar to straight sewing pins, but have a loop at one end. This loop allows you to hang beaded units from the bottom of a soldered pendant or from the main part of an earring design. A simple way to make your own beaded chain is to link eye pins together and attach a clasp. This method can be used to make a very simple soldered necklace chain.

Fishhooks: Sometimes called French wires, these findings have a hook-like shape. They are best used with a plastic nut, which is slipped onto the hook after the earring has been put in place to make sure it does not fall out.

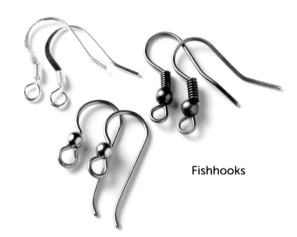

Fishhooks

Head pins: Head pins look similar to straight sewing pins with flat tops instead of sharp points. They can have either flat or decorative bottoms, which are used to keep beads from falling off your earring. They come in every type of metal available on the market.

Hoops: If you want to make a statement with your earrings, hoops will definitely stand out. They can be plain or shaped as semi-circles, from which you can dangle beads and soldered pieces. Plain hoops can also be turned into beaded wine charms.

Leverbacks: Similar in design to fishhooks, these findings have a lever in the back used to close them completely, assuring you that your earring won't fall out. Leverbacks will quickly become one of your favorite earring findings.

Posts: Posts, sometimes referred to as studs, consist of a straight post that is inserted though the ear and secured by a backing or nut. At one time, posts only had a plain ball at the front. Today, posts can have many different motifs to enhance the look of your earrings. Posts can be especially beneficial when you want to make shorter earrings.

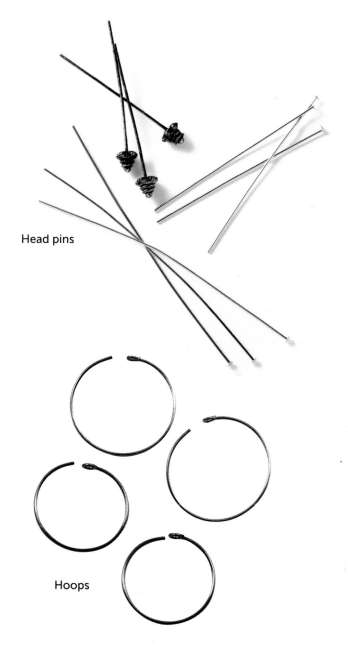

Head pins

Hoops

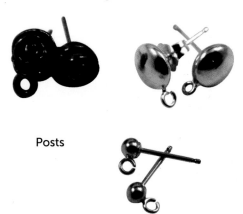

Posts

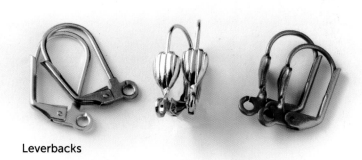

Leverbacks

Soldering Studio
Shopping List

Pre-Soldering Tools
- ❑ Craft scissors
- ❑ Paintbrushes
- ❑ Tweezers
- ❑ Shaped paper hole punches

Pre-Soldering Supplies
- ❑ Glass (pre-cut, stained glass shapes, gems, etc.)
- ❑ Mosaic pieces
- ❑ Broken bits
- ❑ Clip art
- ❑ Decoupage glue
- ❑ Ephemera
- ❑ Markers
- ❑ Paper
- ❑ Photos
- ❑ Stickers or transfers
- ❑ Stamps and inks

Soldering Tools
- ❑ Soldering iron
- ❑ Soldering iron stand
- ❑ Beading tweezers
- ❑ Bone folder
- ❑ File or emery board
- ❑ Flux brush
- ❑ Heat-resistant tile
- ❑ Hemostats
- ❑ Nonstick scissors
- ❑ Rheostat
- ❑ Synthetic sponge
- ❑ Third hand

Soldering Supplies
- ❑ Copper foil tape
- ❑ Flux
- ❑ Glass or multi-purpose cleaner
- ❑ Jump rings
- ❑ Lead-free solder

Jewelry-Making Tools
- ❑ Bent-nose pliers
- ❑ Chain-nose pliers
- ❑ Crimping pliers
- ❑ Flat-nose pliers
- ❑ Round-nose pliers
- ❑ Bead board
- ❑ Bead mat
- ❑ End clamps
- ❑ Wire cutters

Jewelry-Making Supplies
- ❑ Beads
- ❑ Nylon-coated beading wire (medium diameter in 19- or 21-strand count)
- ❑ Clasps
- ❑ 2 x 2mm crimps (either gold-filled or sterling silver)
- ❑ Folded crimps
- ❑ Earring findings
- ❑ Eye pins
- ❑ Head pins

Soldering FAQs

What are the standard sizes of the materials you use for your projects?

Most commonly used glass piece sizes:

Size (U.S.)	Size (Metric)	Shape
1" x 1"	25 x 25mm	Square
1½"	38 x 38mm	Square
1" x 3"	25 x 76mm	Rectangle

Copper foil tape width chart:

Copper foil tape is available in a variety of widths and is sold in 12" x 12" (305 x 305mm) sheets. I most commonly use tape in ³⁄₁₆" (5mm), ⁷⁄₃₂" (5.5mm), ¼" (6mm), and ⁵⁄₁₆" (8mm) widths.

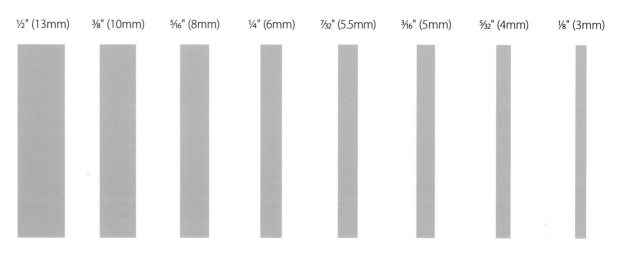

½" (13mm) ⅜" (10mm) ⁵⁄₁₆" (8mm) ¼" (6mm) ⁷⁄₃₂" (5.5mm) ³⁄₁₆" (5mm) ⁵⁄₃₂" (4mm) ⅛" (3mm)

Bead Size Chart

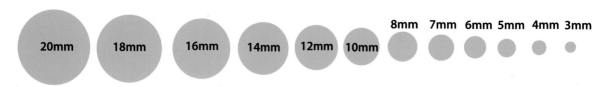

20mm 18mm 16mm 14mm 12mm 10mm 8mm 7mm 6mm 5mm 4mm 3mm

What is a sal ammoniac (ammonium chloride) block, and should I use one?

Sal ammoniac or tinning blocks can be used to clean the tip of your soldering iron. However, if you regularly clean your iron with a sponge, this product is unnecessary. Sal ammoniac blocks can also give off toxic fumes and should therefore only be used in well-ventilated areas. Because of this, I don't recommend sal ammoniac or tinning blocks for beginners.

What if I start a project and can't finish it in one session?

Sometimes life gets in the way, and you may not be able to complete your soldered project in one sitting. If you have already wrapped your project in copper foil, store it in a plastic bag to prevent the copper from oxidizing. Oxidized copper does not allow solder to stick to its surface. Partially soldered projects with flux already applied to the surface of the copper foil should have the flux cleaned off and be stored in a plastic bag.

How can I make the shine on my solder last?

The shine of freshly applied solder is so pretty, but time and oxygen can take a toll and dull the look of your finished piece. For long-lasting shine, try buffing the solder with carnauba wax. The wax will keep oxygen from reaching the metal and dulling its surface.

Help, my solder looks lumpy! Is there anything I can do?

Take a deep breath! One of the great things about solder is that it can be melted over and over. Smooth out any rough areas by applying a little flux to the uneven spot. Without adding any solder to the tip of your iron, hold your soldering iron against the section you want to fix. As it heats up, the metal will eventually liquefy, giving you the opportunity to smooth it. To smooth away a small burr or lump, use a file or emery board.

Simple Steps for Making Soldered Jewelry

Now that you are well versed in the tools and materials you need to make a soldered piece of jewelry, it's time to put those tools to use and start creating. This chapter contains some simple step-by-step projects to help you on your way. The first project shows you how to assemble a simple pendant, solder it, and attach a jump ring so the pendant can be used in a necklace design. If this is your first soldering project, don't worry if it's not perfect. Consider this a practice session. Following the soldering project are two additional projects that walk you through creating two simple jewelry designs you can use to show off a soldered piece.

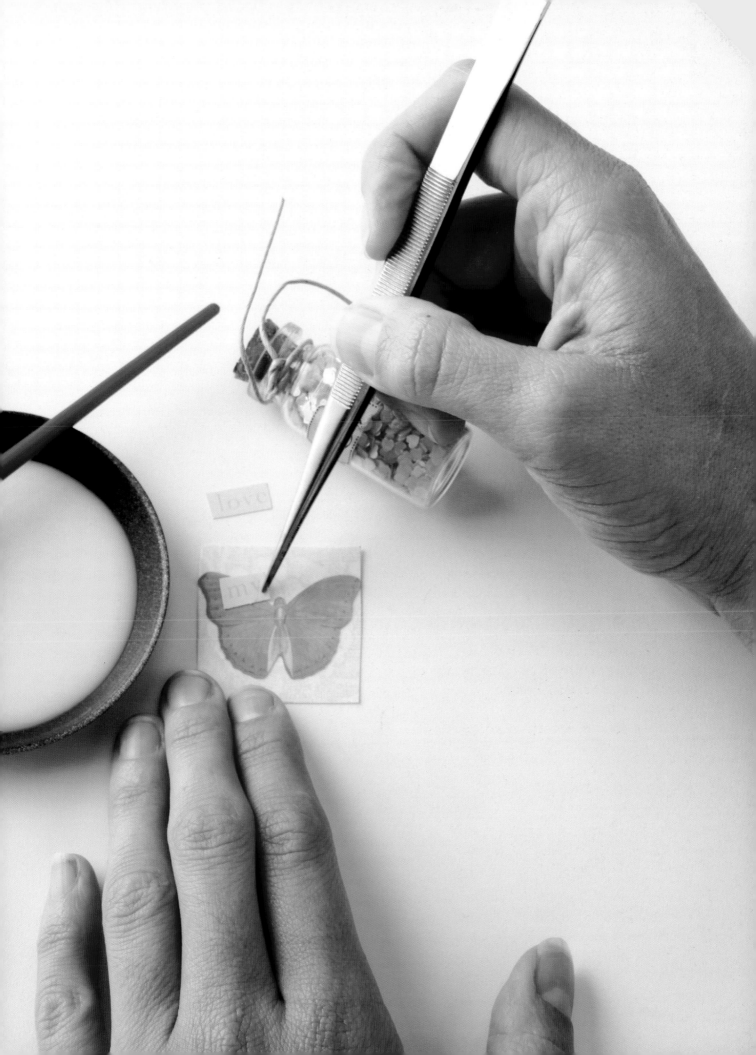

Basic Soldered Pendant

Once you learn how to make a basic soldered pendant, you'll be able to solder almost anything. Pendants make great focal pieces for necklaces and bracelets and can be scaled down for use in earring designs. And remember that you can use almost anything you can get your hands on in a soldering project!

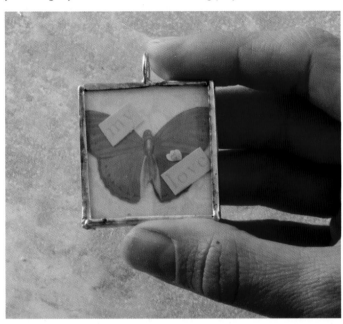

Tools and materials:

- ❏ Soldering tools and supplies (see page 39)
- ❏ One 16- to 18-gauge jump ring
- ❏ Two identical glass pieces
- ❏ Decorative or colored paper of choice (background)
- ❏ Assorted ephemera
- ❏ Damp sponge
- ❏ Craft scissors
- ❏ Marker or pen
- ❏ Tweezers
- ❏ Paper
- ❏ Paintbrushes
- ❏ Decoupage glue

The author used these products for the project. Substitute your choice of brands, tools, and materials as desired.

Assemble the jewelry component

1 **Trace the glass.** Place one of the glass pieces on a sheet of decorative or colored paper of your choice. Using the marker, trace the shape of the glass onto the paper.

2 **Cut the background.** Using small, sharp craft scissors, cut just inside the lines you drew during Step 1. The cutout will become the background for your jewelry component.

3 **Assemble your ephemera.** Gather the assorted ephemera, photos, or other items you would like to use to assemble your jewelry component. For this project, I used the image of a butterfly, two small pieces of paper with a word printed on each one, and some tiny paper hearts.

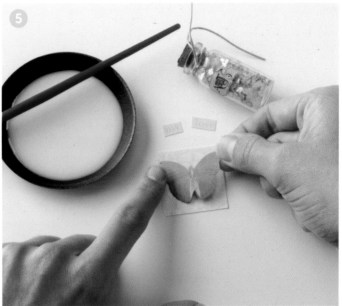

4 **Glue the ephemera.** Select one of your items from Step 3. Using a paintbrush, cover the entire back surface with decoupage glue.

5 **Attach the ephemera.** Take the item you glued during the previous step and align it over your background paper. Press it in place. You can choose to center the item or place it in any other manner you desire. Repeat Steps 4 and 5 to glue any other large items to your background paper.

6 **Attach any small items.** If you would like to add some small elements to your design, like the small pieces of paper I incorporated in my pendant, use beading tweezers to hold the item as you apply glue, and then use the tweezers to position and place the glued piece.

Suzann's Sensational Soldering Tip

Once you have glued all items to your piece of background paper, use the shovel end of your beading tweezers to help flatten and smooth the glued pieces. This will keep the finished piece from getting wrinkled and lumpy as the glue dries.

7 **Encase the project.** After the assembly has dried, place it between the two glass pieces. Use the scissors to trim away any paper that extends beyond the edges of the glass. This ensures the copper foil will lie flat against the edges of the glass when you wrap your piece.

Altered Glass

One medium that is often overlooked when creating soldered pieces is the glass itself. By altering the surface of the glass you're using for a project, you can add a whole new dimension to your piece. Try a few of the following techniques to give your pieces a different look.

Acrylic paint: Use stencils, brushes, and stamps to apply acrylic paint to the inside surface of your glass pieces.

Archival ink and stamps: Archival ink is specially formulated to adhere to non-porous surfaces like glass. It is also waterproof.

Sanding: A simple emery board, nail file, or piece of sandpaper can give your glass an aged look. Vary the pressure you use to produce a lightly distressed look or an extremely distressed look.

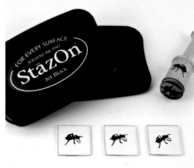

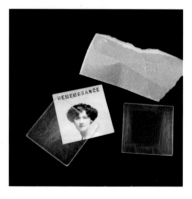

Solder the jewelry component

8 **Size the copper foil tape.** Use your jewelry component to measure the amount of copper foil you will need by loosely wrapping it around your glass-encased project. Use nonstick scissors to trim off the appropriate amount. After some practice, you might be able to wrap your project in copper foil straight from the roll.

9 **Remove the backing.** Peel away approximately ½" (13mm) of the paper backing from the copper foil. Removing the backing in small sections makes it easier to handle the copper foil tape.

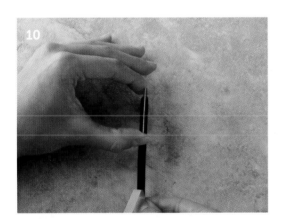

Suzann's Sensational Soldering Tip

Before you start wrapping copper foil tape around your assembly, take the time to clean both sides of the glass pieces. This way, everyone will see your beautiful work instead of your fingerprints!

10 **Center the assembly.** Place the top edge of your glass-encased assembly in the center of the exposed tape. Align it so there is an even border of tape along each side. Peel away an additional section of backing from the tape and rotate the assembly to cover the next edge in tape. Continue carefully wrapping the edges of the assembly in tape until all four edges are covered. Make sure the project is always centered on the tape.

11 **Secure the tape.** Secure the tape to the assembly by placing a small portion of the finishing end of the tape over the starting end of the tape. This overlapping will seal the ends of the copper foil tape together.

12 **Fold over the tape.** Use your fingers to wrap the portions of the copper foil tape that extend past the edges of your assembly down onto the glass. Use your fingernail to crease the corners so the tape lies flat. Fold the tape down on both the front and back glass pieces.

13 **Burnish the tape.** Use the bone folder to burnish the tape with firm, but gentle, pressure. This ensures the tape is properly adhered to the glass and helps remove any wrinkles that may have been created during wrapping and folding. Turn on your soldering iron and allow it to warm up as you complete this step.

Suzann's Sensational Soldering Tip

Apply a nice, even layer of flux to the copper foil tape. Too much flux can sometimes cause the solder to spit or pop. Wipe the brush on the edge of your container to control the amount of flux you are using.

14 **Apply flux.** Using your flux brush, apply a thin layer of flux to the surface of the copper foil tape.

15 **Prepare the solder and iron.** Once your iron is properly heated, wipe the tip on the moistened sponge to clean it. Then, unwrap and trim a small section of solder from a roll.

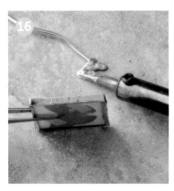

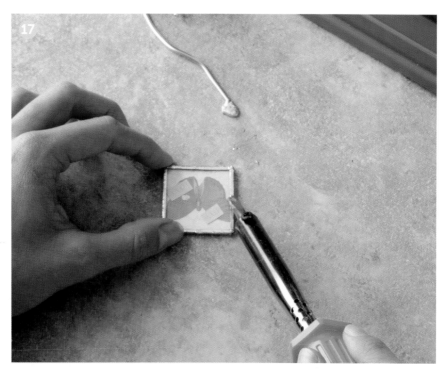

16 **Pick up the solder.** Hold the tip of your soldering iron against one end of the section of solder you cut during the previous step. When the solder begins to liquefy, pick it up by rolling the soldering iron, covering the tip with the molten metal.

17 **Apply solder to the front and back.** With the solder on the tip of your soldering iron, place the tip of the iron against the copper foil tape on the front face of the assembly. Slowly move the tip along the copper foil. You will see the solder affix itself to the copper foil. Use this process to add solder to the copper foil on the front of your project. When the solder has cooled, use tweezers to flip the assembly over and apply solder to the back. WARNING: Liquefied solder is extremely hot. Keep your fingers away from your project as you apply solder. If you need to pick up or move your project, use tweezers. Here, I am holding my pendant while soldering for illustration purposes only. Use your tweezers to hold your project while soldering.

18 **Apply solder to the edges.** After you have added solder to the back, grasp the assembly with your tweezers and hold it with one of the edges facing up. Apply solder to each outer edge of the assembly. Only use your tweezers to handle your project.

Suzann's Sensational Soldering Tip

You may need to add multiple layers of solder to your assembly to achieve the final look you want. Add the same number of layers to each edge of the assembly to maintain an even appearance.

Attach a jump ring

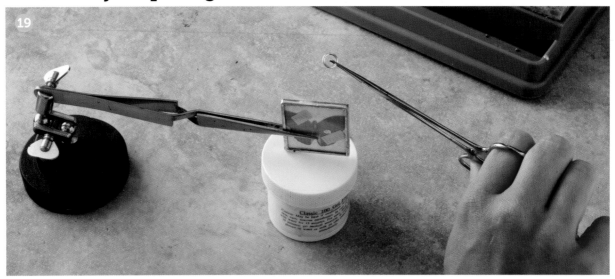

19 **Prepare the assembly and jump ring.** Place your soldered jewelry component in a third hand. Grip a jump ring in the jaws of a hemostat and lock the jaws in position. Make sure the opening of the jump ring is facing out.

20 **Apply flux.** Brush the opening of the jump ring and the opposite edge of the ring (the edge you will attach to your jewelry component) with flux.

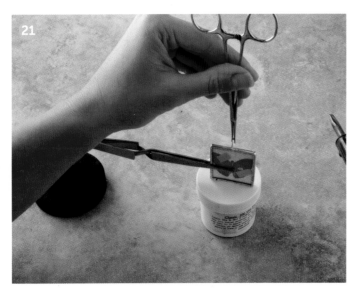

21 **Position the jump ring.** Holding the hemostat in one hand, position your jump ring, centering it along the top edge of your jewelry component. Make sure the opening of the jump ring is pointing straight up.

Suzann's Sensational Soldering Tip

Changing the color of the solder on a finished piece used to involve harsh, toxic chemicals. Today, there are plenty of safe and effective ways to color your silver solder. Gilders paste, paint pens, permanent markers, acrylic paint, and inkpads can all be used to create a unique, colorful effect.

22 **Apply solder.** Holding the hemostat with the jump ring in place with one hand, use your other hand to pick up your soldering iron. Press the tip of your soldering iron against the solder to one side of the jump ring for a few seconds, warming the solder. Repeat on the other side of the jump ring. Continue alternately warming the solder on both sides of the jump ring until the solder begins to liquefy.

23 **Place the jump ring.** As you heat the solder, you will feel the jump ring sink into the liquid metal. When this happens, remove the soldering iron and let the solder cool around the jump ring.

24 **Remove the hemostat.** Once the solder has completely cooled and solidified around your jump ring, unlock and remove the hemostat. You have now created a captivating pendant that can be featured in a necklace or bracelet design.

Simple Dangle Earrings

This project shows you how to make a simple set of dangle earrings. To incorporate soldered pieces into this design, create two small, identical soldered pieces and attach a jump ring to the top of each one. Follow the steps below to create a set of dangle earrings using beads that match your soldered components. Use the jump rings at the tops of your soldered pieces to attach them to the base of each earring. Note: To add soldered components to this earring design, you will need to use eye pins instead of head pins.

Tools and materials:

- ❑ Round-nose pliers
- ❑ Chain-nose pliers
- ❑ Wire cutters
- ❑ Bead mat
- ❑ Pair of earring findings (leverbacks, fishhooks, or posts)
- ❑ Head pins (eye pins if attaching soldered pendants)
- ❑ Beads of choice
- ❑ Soldered components

The author used these products for the project. Substitute your choice of brands, tools, and materials as desired.

1 Arrange your beads on the head pin as you would like them (use an eye pin if adding soldered components). When adding your beads, remember to leave at least ½" (13mm) of the top of the head pin exposed so you can make a loop. When you're just starting out, you might find it easier to leave a longer length of the pin exposed, as shown here.

2 **Bend the head pin.** Using your chain-nose pliers, bend the exposed top of the head pin at a 90-degree angle, flush against the top bead of your design.

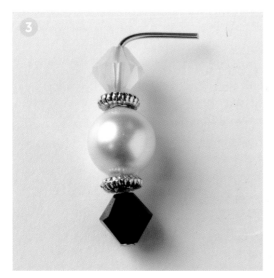

3 **Trim the head pin.** Cut the exposed head pin wire down to ¼" (6mm).

4 **Go "tip to tip."** Use the area close to the tip of your round-nose pliers to grasp the tip of the head pin.

5 **Form a loop.** Twist your wrist to roll up and over with your pliers to form a loop out of the tip of your head pin.

6 **Attach the finding.** Swing the loop open—don't pull. Attach your earring finding and swing the loop closed. Make sure the ends of your loop fit together tightly, so it does not fall off your earring finding.

7 **Attach soldered components.** If you would like to incorporate soldered pendants into your earring design, use your round-nose and chain-nose pliers to open the jump ring attached to a soldered piece. Slip the open jump ring onto the loop at the base of your earring and close the jump ring.

Suzann's Sensational Soldering Tip

The twist of your wrist used to make a loop is very similar to that of turning a can opener.

Using a Jump Ring

It is very important that you learn to open and close a jump ring properly, or it can lose its shape and come apart later. You will need round-nose pliers, chain-nose pliers, and a jump ring.

 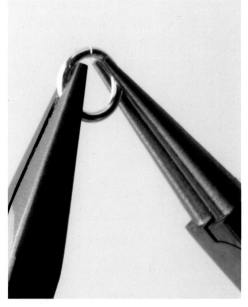

Open the jump ring

Step 1: Take the chain-nose pliers in your left hand and, using the jaws, pick up your jump ring on the left-hand side close to the opening so that the opening is facing up.

Step 2: In your right hand, pick up the round-nose pliers and grasp the right side of the jump ring near the opening with the jaws. The jump ring should now be held by both sets of pliers.

Step 3: Slowly twist the sides of the jump ring in opposite directions to open it, one hand with the pliers moving forward and the other backward. The key is to twist, not pull. If a jump ring is pulled apart, the circle of the metal will become misshapen and will not close properly.

Close the jump ring

Step 1: Place the pliers back on either side of the opening and twist the ends back toward the center, letting them pass each other just a little bit.

Step 2: Twist the ends back to the center. You will know the jump ring is properly closed when you feel the two ends rub together or hear a little click. You may have to wiggle back and forth a few times and push the two sides in slightly with the pliers while the ends are passing one another to get the jump ring completely closed.

Simple Bracelet or Necklace with Crimps

The following steps teach you how to fashion a simple bracelet or necklace design. To incorporate a soldered piece, use a soldered pendant as the focal point of the design and select beads to match it. You can easily adapt this design to make a charm bracelet by using several small soldered pendants throughout the design.

Tools and materials:

- ❏ Crimping pliers
- ❏ Wire cutters
- ❏ Bead board
- ❏ Bead mat
- ❏ End clamp
- ❏ Beading wire
- ❏ Clasp
- ❏ 2 x 2mm crimps
- ❏ Beads
- ❏ Soldered components

The author used these products for the project. Substitute your choice of brands, tools, and materials as desired.

1 Arrange your beads. Organize your beads (and soldered components if desired) on a bead board to design your jewelry composition. Remember, the center of your design will always be at the number zero on the bead board. This means if you are incorporating a soldered pendant into your design, place it at zero on the bead board. If using a multi-channel bead board, only use the outside track when measuring the piece. This will give you the correct measurement in inches.

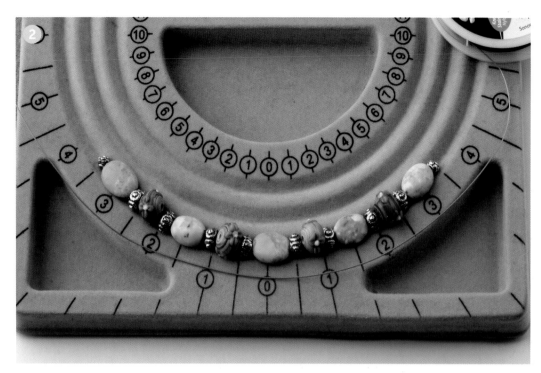

2 **Measure and cut the wire.** Once you are happy with your design, take your beading wire and measure your design on the bead board. Add an additional 4" (102mm) to the total length of the wire and cut it. The extra wire will ensure you have enough at either end of your design when you are ready to attach your clasp.

3 **Attach an end clamp.** Place an end clamp 2" (51mm) from one end of the wire. The end clamp will keep your beads from falling off the wire while you are stringing them.

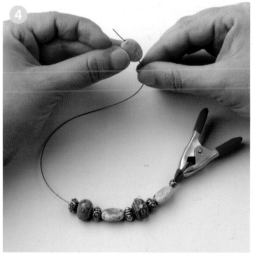

4 **String the components.** String your beads (and soldered components as desired) onto the wire. You may want to lay your piece back down on the bead board once you have placed the components. Designs can sometimes look different or be a different length once strung.

5 **String one crimp and half the clasp.** Once you are done stringing your last bead, string on one crimp tube. Next, string on one half of your clasp.

6 **Secure the clasp.** Feed the wire back through the crimp, pulling it tightly so the clasp is snugly held in the loop created by the wire. Make sure the crimp tube is flush against the last bead with no wire showing.

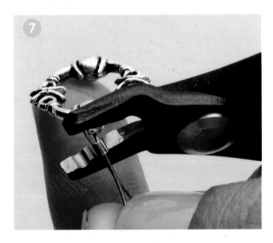

7 **Prepare to close the crimp tube.** Grab your crimping pliers. You will see two half circles located in the lower jaw. Position the pliers around the crimp tube, using the half circle that is closest to your hand.

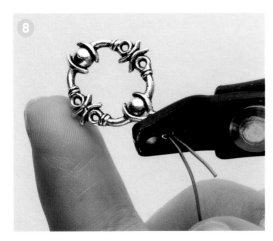

8 **Make the first crimp.** Make sure the wires that are threaded through the crimp tube are not crossed. Squeeze the pliers firmly and then open the jaws. You should see two u-shaped channels in the crimp tube.

9 **Prepare for the second crimp.** Take the crimp tube and put it in the half circle of the crimping pliers that is furthest from your hand. Stand it up so that the two channels you just made are facing you.

10 **Make the second crimp.** Squeeze the pliers together so the crimp tube folds and the two channels in the tube meet.

11 **Trim the wire and finish.** Cut the wire tail as close to the crimp tube as possible with your wire cutters. Turn your design over to the unfinished end. Remove the end clamp and repeat steps 5–10 with the other half of the clasp.

4

Soldered Jewelry Designs

Now that you've created your first soldered pendant and have learned how to incorporate soldered components into your jewelry designs, it's time to take your skills to the next level. Use the information you've learned about soldering from the previous chapters and apply it to make any number of the following projects that inspire you. Remember, this is about you creating jewelry that you love and that suits your taste. If you'd like to alter a design to make it better fit your personality, do it! With soldering and jewelry design, there are countless options and endless possibilities, so don't be afraid to tap into your creativity. These projects are just a sampling of what you can do with soldering.

Ants Go Marching, page 76.

Pendants

Pendants are perfect projects to build up your soldering skills. They can be used in practically any piece of jewelry, from necklaces and earrings to bracelets and anklets. You can even use pendants to create customized gift tags or wine glass charms. And because the pendants are made from materials you have selected, they will always have your special touch.

Feeling Green

Who knew recycling could be so eye catching? Feeling Green is a perfect example how broken can still be beautiful. Shattered pottery, like the piece used for this pendant, can often be rescued and turned into a stunning focal piece for a knockout necklace.

Tools and materials:

- ❑ Soldering tools and supplies (see page 39)
- ❑ 5" (127mm) of ⅝" (16mm)-wide copper foil tape
- ❑ 1 green pottery shard used for mosaics
- ❑ One 16- or 18-gauge jump ring

The author used these products for the project. Substitute your choice of brands, tools, and materials as desired.

Use the method described in the step-by-step project on page 44 to wrap the pottery shard with the copper foil tape, apply solder, and add a jump ring. Note: You are wrapping the pottery shard in the tape; there is no need to sandwich it in glass. Once your pendant is complete, design a necklace to feature your creation.

Flights of Memory

Mixing various types of craft media enables you to combine materials that aren't often paired together and turn them into a creation that is both bold and beautiful. Flights of Memory blends clip art, a small scrap piece of WireKnitZ jewelry mesh, the word "memory" torn from a piece of scrapbooking embellishment tape, and a scrap piece of blue artisan paper in a pendant that is hard to forget!

Tools and materials:

- ❑ Soldering tools and supplies (see page 39)
- ❑ 2 pieces of 1½" (38mm)-square memory glass
- ❑ 7½" (191mm) of ⁵⁄₁₆" (8mm)-wide wavy copper foil tape
- ❑ One 16- to 18-gauge jump ring
- ❑ Craft scissors
- ❑ Decoupage glue and brush
- ❑ 1½" (38mm) square of blue artisan paper
- ❑ 1" (25mm) square of bird clip art
- ❑ 1 "Memory" word
- ❑ ⅛" x ¹⁄₁₆" (3 x 2mm) WireKnitZ jewelry mesh in raspberry

The author used these products for the project. Substitute your choice of brands, tools, and materials as desired.

Use the method described in the step-by-step project on page 44 to sandwich the artisan paper, clip art, "memory" word, and jewelry mesh between the squares of memory glass. Wrap the assembly in the wavy copper foil tape, apply solder, and attach the jump ring.

Suzann's Sensational Soldering Tip

Save those scraps. If you have little bits of leftover creative goodies from another project, hang on to them. You can pull them out later and use them to create mixed-media pendants.

Shine On!

Recently, artist Martin M. Rocha was honored with a first place win at the Chicago Fest for Beatles Fans for his pencil rendering of John Lennon on a fictitious Spanish Rolling Stone *magazine cover. Shine On! was designed to commemorate Martin's shining moment, but any classic rock aficionado would wear it with pride!*

Tools and materials:

- ❏ Soldering tools and supplies (see page 39)
- ❏ Two 1" x 3" (25 x 76mm) pieces of memory glass
- ❏ 9" (229mm) of ½" (13mm)-wide black-backed copper foil tape
- ❏ One 1" x 3" (25 x 76mm) section from John Lennon drawing by Martin M. Rocha
- ❏ 1 "Imagine" word
- ❏ Decoupage glue and brush
- ❏ Edging scissors with ripple blade
- ❏ Craft scissors

The author used these products for the project. Substitute your choice of brands, tools, and materials as desired.

Suzann's Sensational Soldering Tip

You can customize the edges of your copper foil tape like I did for the *Shine On!* Pendant using edging scissors or edge punches. You can find a wide variety of these in the scrapbooking section of your local craft store.

Treasure

A simple glass bottle becomes a real treasure with a few small additions. By placing items inside the bottle and soldering around the top, your treasures will be safe for all time. The bottle I used comes with a jump ring already attached to the cork. You can find these at most major craft stores.

Tools and materials:

- ❑ Soldering tools and supplies (see page 39)
- ❑ Glass bottle with jump ring cork stopper
- ❑ Miniature key charm
- ❑ Miniature treasure map
- ❑ 3 pearl beads
- ❑ Black sand
- ❑ 1 "Treasure" word
- ❑ Decoupage glue and brush
- ❑ 2" (51mm) of ⁵⁄₁₆" (8mm)-wide copper foil tape

The author used these products for the project. Substitute your choice of brands, tools, and materials as desired.

Fill your glass bottle with the key charm, treasure map, pearls, sand, and any additional items you desire. Insert the cork. Wrap the upper lip of the glass bottle in the copper foil tape and apply solder.

Passion

Passion is in full bloom with this pendant. The project you see is actually the opposite side of the Marylyn Monroe pendant featured in the Hollywood Glamor *project in my previous book* Simple Beginnings: Beading. *The image was produced on a computer by typing text over a flower photo to create the final design. I then resized the image to fit inside the memory glass pieces I used for the pendant.*

Use the computer, printer, and clip art software to create a photo for the pendant. You can recreate my design or make something that is completely your own. Print your image at 1½" x 1½" (38 x 38mm) on the photo paper, place it between the memory glass pieces, and solder.

Tools and materials:

- ❑ Soldering tools and supplies (see page 39)
- ❑ 7" (178mm) of ¼" (6mm)-wide copper foil tape
- ❑ Two 1½" (38mm)-square memory glass pieces
- ❑ Computer and printer
- ❑ Clip art or word processing software
- ❑ 1 sheet of 8.5" x 11" (216 x 279mm) matte photo paper
- ❑ One 16- or 18-gauge jump ring
- ❑ Craft scissors

The author used these products for the project. Substitute your choice of brands, tools, and materials as desired.

Sizzlin' Hot

This sassy pendant may look complex and pricy, but it is unbelievably easy and inexpensive to make! A tile from your local home improvement store rubbed across a red inkpad creates the backdrop for vintage clip art and scrapbook word stickers. Cover the finished design with sealant to make sure the colors stay put while you are frolicking on the beach.

Tools and materials:

- ❑ Soldering tools and supplies (see page 39)
- ❑ ¼" (6mm)-wide copper foil tape
- ❑ One 1" x 2½" (25 x 64mm) ceramic tile
- ❑ One 16- or 18-gauge jump ring
- ❑ 1 red inkpad
- ❑ Craft scissors
- ❑ 1 clip art image
- ❑ Scrapbook word stickers (or use paper cutouts of words)
- ❑ Decoupage glue and brush
- ❑ Sealant

The author used these products for the project. Substitute your choice of brands, tools, and materials as desired.

Allow the ink on the tile to dry completely before gluing the clip art on top. Spray the finished tile with a couple coats of sealant before soldering to make sure the ink does not fade or run.

World Traveler

Recount your travels abroad by making this World Traveler pendant. No matter where you go, the beauty of this design is sure to get complements. Use the method from the previous project to add paper elements to the ceramic tile, apply sealant, and solder the edges.

Tools and materials:

- ❑ Soldering tools and supplies (see page 39)
- ❑ ¼" (6mm)-wide black-backed copper foil tape
- ❑ One 1" x 2½" (25 x 64mm) ceramic tile
- ❑ One 16- or 18-gauge jump ring
- ❑ 1 pink inkpad
- ❑ Craft scissors
- ❑ 1 postage stamp sticker
- ❑ 1 "Travel" word
- ❑ 1 small map piece
- ❑ Decoupage glue and brush
- ❑ Glitter acrylic paint for sealant

The author used these products for the project. Substitute your choice of brands, tools, and materials as desired.

Necklaces

Necklaces are a wonderful way to show off your newfound soldering talents to the world. This section shows you several different necklace design ideas that range from elegant to playful. Recreate them in your soldering studio or adapt the designs to feature you own original soldered components. No matter how you wish to express yourself, the necklace you create from your soldered pieces will make sure you stand out from the crowd!

Ancient Glass

The design for this necklace might look complicated, but it only takes minutes to make! The green glass pieces come pre-packaged and are available in the mosaic section of your local craft store. Simply apply solder to the edges of each mosaic square, add a jump ring to the right and left sides of each piece, connect the pieces with additional jump rings, and add a clasp. You will be pleasantly surprised by how quickly this necklace comes together.

Tools and materials:

- ❏ Soldering tools and supplies (see page 39)
- ❏ 13 green mosaic glass squares
- ❏ Forty 16- or 18-gauge jump rings (26 attached to the sides of the mosaic squares, 14 used as connectors between the soldered components)
- ❏ 1 S-hook clasp
- ❏ ⁵⁄₁₆" (8mm)-wide copper foil tape
- ❏ Round-nose pliers
- ❏ Chain-nose pliers

The author used these products for the project. Substitute your choice of brands, tools, and materials as desired.

Siren's Song

The pendant on this necklace was made using a glass "stone" that can be found in the floral department of your local craft store. The bubble-like dome of the glass piece helps enhance the ocean theme of this necklace by slightly distorting the mermaid image, as objects under water appear distorted when viewed from the surface. The use of abalone beads continues the maritime theme and makes this a pretty piece any mermaid would desire.

Tools and materials:

- ❑ Soldering tools and supplies (see page 39)
- ❑ Mermaid clip art image from Nunn Designs
- ❑ Craft scissors
- ❑ Copper foil tape sheet cut to size
- ❑ ¼" (6mm)-wide black-backed copper foil tape
- ❑ 1 flat-backed glass "stone"
- ❑ 10 oval abalone beads
- ❑ 8 silver disk-shaped spacers
- ❑ 4 silver spheres
- ❑ 2 Bali-style silver spheres
- ❑ 18 quartz beads
- ❑ Two 2 x 2mm crimp tubes
- ❑ 1 toggle clasp
- ❑ One 16- or 18-gauge jump ring
- ❑ Beading wire
- ❑ Crimping pliers
- ❑ Wire cutters

The author used these products for the project. Substitute your choice of brands, tools, and materials as desired.

Place your glass stone on the back of the copper foil tape sheet, trace around it, and cut out the shape. Place your image on the back of the stone. Then, remove the backing from the copper foil tape cutout and place it over the back of the image, wrapping the sides up around the stone as needed. Wrap the edge of the stone in the ¼" (6mm) copper foil tape. Apply solder to all the copper foil areas and attach a jump ring.

Flower Power

Bring a burst of color into your wardrobe with this Flower Power necklace. Paint the back of one of the glass pieces with acrylic paint, using a paper floral border as a stencil. The paper you place inside the pendant will peek through the unpainted part of the glass to give added dimension to the piece. Try different paint, stencil, and paper combinations to stretch your creativity.

Tools and materials:

- ❑ Soldering tools and supplies (see page 39)
- ❑ 9" (229mm) of ¼" (6mm)-wide black-backed copper foil tape
- ❑ One 1" x 3" (25 x 76mm) piece of scrapbook paper
- ❑ Two 1" x 3" (25 x 76mm) microscope slides
- ❑ One 16- or 18-gauge jump ring
- ❑ Acrylic paint in turquoise and yellow
- ❑ Paintbrushes
- ❑ Craft scissors
- ❑ One 3" (76mm)-long floral border
- ❑ 30 turquoise beads
- ❑ 8 silver daisy spacers
- ❑ 20" (508mm) of 19- or 21-strand flexible beading wire
- ❑ 2 crimp tubes
- ❑ 1 toggle clasp
- ❑ Crimping pliers
- ❑ Wire cutters

The author used these products for the project. Substitute your choice of brands, tools, and materials as desired.

Vintage Photography

Some of the best pendants you create will express your passions, interests, or special memories. The clip art used in the Vintage Photography *necklace was chosen to convey the love of photography shared by my Dad and me. Make your next soldering project a gift that highlights a special interest of the recipient.*

Tools and materials:

- ❑ Soldering tools and supplies (see page 39)
- ❑ One 1½" (38mm) square of vintage clip art
- ❑ Craft scissors
- ❑ Two 1½" (38mm)-square memory glass pieces
- ❑ 5⁄16" (8mm)-wide copper foil tape
- ❑ One 16- or 18-gauge jump ring
- ❑ 12 oval quartz beads
- ❑ 14 striped saucer beads
- ❑ 6 silver spheres
- ❑ Two 2 x 2mm crimp tubes
- ❑ 1 toggle clasp
- ❑ Beading wire
- ❑ Crimping pliers
- ❑ Wire cutters

The author used these products for the project. Substitute your choice of brands, tools, and materials as desired.

Fresh Picked

The bloom inside this pendant is actually made of fabric. I added a jump ring to the bottom of the piece so I could attach a matching beaded dangle. The flat-backed aquamarine rhinestone is glued over the center of the fabric flower on the outside of the top glass piece to give it a little extra sparkle and dimension.

Tools and materials:

- ❑ Soldering tools and supplies (see page 39)
- ❑ 7" (178mm) of ⁵⁄₁₆" (8mm)-wide copper foil tape
- ❑ Scrapbook paper
- ❑ Fabric flower
- ❑ Bead in coordinating colors
- ❑ 1 aquamarine flat-backed rhinestone
- ❑ Jewelry glue
- ❑ Decoupage glue and brush
- ❑ Craft scissors
- ❑ Two 1½" (38mm)-square memory glass pieces
- ❑ 4 jump rings (2 for pendant, 2 for clasp)
- ❑ Green ribbon
- ❑ 2 folded crimp tubes
- ❑ 1 lobster claw clasp
- ❑ Chain-nose pliers
- ❑ Flat-nose pliers
- ❑ Round-nose pliers

The author used these products for the project. Substitute your choice of brands, tools, and materials as desired.

When you are ready to attach your clasp to your necklace, take one end of ribbon and lay it inside one of the open folded crimp tubes. Gently bend one half of the folded crimp over the end of the ribbon using your flat-nose pliers. Bend the second half of the folded crimp over the first half. For extra security, add a dab of jewelry glue if desired. Repeat with the remaining crimp on the other end of the ribbon. Use jump rings to attach each half of the clasp to the folded crimps.

Calming Waters

Bring yourself to a place of tranquility with the soothing colors of this necklace design.

Tools and materials:

❑ Soldering tools and supplies (see page 39)

❑ One 1" x 3" (25 x 76mm) ceramic tile

❑ Copper foil tape sheet

❑ Dragonfly paper punch

❑ Craft scissors

❑ 1 "Calm" word

❑ Turquoise inkpad

❑ Decoupage glue and brush

❑ ¼" (6mm)-wide copper foil tape

❑ One 16- or 18-gauge jump ring

❑ 54 turquoise oval beads

❑ 6 silver pebble-shaped beads

❑ 12 silver spacers

❑ Two 2 x 2mm crimp tubes

❑ 1 toggle clasp

❑ Beading wire

❑ Crimping pliers

❑ Wire cutters

The author used these products for the project. Substitute your choice of brands, tools, and materials as desired.

You can make the dragonfly for this pendant by cutting it from a piece of colored or patterned paper with a dragonfly-shaped hole punch. To make a soldered dragonfly like the one pictured, punch the dragonfly from a copper foil sheet. Attach the copper foil dragonfly to the front of the pendant and cover it in solder.

Bracelets

Soldered components can really make your bracelets pop. Larger pendants can be used as a focal piece for the center of a bracelet design, or you can join soldered components together with jump rings to create a piece that really accentuates your skills. Either way, your bracelets will have people asking, "Where did you get that?" Now you can proudly say, "I made it!"

Steampunk Time

Get yourself geared up with this watch-style steampunk bracelet. I created the dial by stamping the image onto a piece of canvas paper. Linking the gears together using jump rings gives this bracelet just the right industrial, chic look.

Tools and materials:

- ❑ Soldering tools and supplies (see page 39)
- ❑ Two 1" (25mm)-square memory glass pieces
- ❑ 1 clock dial stamp
- ❑ Brown inkpad
- ❑ Craft scissors
- ❑ One 1" (25mm) square of canvas scrapbook paper
- ❑ 6 gears in various shapes and sizes (more if needed to increase bracelet size)
- ❑ Eleven 16- or 18-gauge jump rings
- ❑ 1 lobster claw clasp
- ❑ Chain-nose pliers
- ❑ Round-nose pliers

The author used these products for the project. Substitute your choice of brands, tools, and materials as desired.

Ants Go Marching

You won't mind having your picnic invaded by these cute visitors! The ants are stamped on the inside of the glass to create a pseudo 3-D effect. Each of the soldered pieces has an ant stamped on one side and a flower sticker on the other. The wearer can rotate the tiles so all the ants are showing at once, all the flowers are showing at once, or a mix of the two. This bracelet is a fun way to enjoy a warm summer day!

Tools and materials:

- ❏ Soldering tools and supplies (see page 39)
- ❏ Six 1" (25mm)-square memory glass pieces
- ❏ Three 1" squares of scrapbook paper
- ❏ Black archival ink
- ❏ Ant stamp
- ❏ 3 flower stickers
- ❏ Craft scissors
- ❏ Eight 16- or 18-gauge jump rings (6 for the soldered pieces, 2 for the clasp)
- ❏ Four 10mm red Czech fire-polished beads
- ❏ 4 silver eye pins
- ❏ 1 toggle clasp
- ❏ Round-nose pliers
- ❏ Chain-nose pliers

The author used these products for the project. Substitute your choice of brands, tools, and materials as desired.

Thread the four eye pins through each of the four beads. Use your pliers to create a loop at the straight end of each eye pin to hold the bead in place. Attach the loops of each end of the eye pins to the jump rings on the end of the soldered pieces and clasp.

Heart on My Sleeve

Wearing your heart on your sleeve can be a gorgeous thing!

Wrap the sides of the heart gem in copper foil tape and apply solder. Attach three jump rings to each side of the heart. Take a length of beading wire and thread it through the top jump ring on one side of the heart. Use a crimp tube to secure the wire in place. Repeat with the remaining strands of beading wire and jump rings on the heart. Thread beads onto each of the strands of beading wire. String twelve silver beads onto the top strands on both sides of the heart. String fourteen silver beads onto the bottom strands on both sides of the heart. For the middle strand on each side, alternate the bicone crystals and the briolettes. Before attaching the clasp, braid the three strands of beads on each side of the heart together. Then, use crimps to secure the strands to the clasp halves.

Tools and materials:

- ❏ Soldering tools and supplies (see page 39)
- ❏ Large glass heart gem
- ❏ Six 16- or 18-gauge jump rings
- ❏ 12 crimp tubes
- ❏ 6 lengths of beading wire
- ❏ 1 triple-strand clasp
- ❏ ½" (13mm)-wide copper foil tape
- ❏ 52 silver spheres
- ❏ 8 black bicone spacers
- ❏ 6 burgundy briolettes
- ❏ Crimping pliers
- ❏ Wire cutters

The author used these products for the project. Substitute your choice of brands, tools, and materials as desired.

Other Jewelry

Ready to use some of your soldering talents in new ways? Try making some of these other types of jewelry to expand your creativity and expertise!

Cut a piece of the copper foil tape sheet to cover the back of the gem. Attach the scrapbook paper to the gem, attach copper foil to the back and sides, and apply solder. Color the solder as desired using a marker or paint pen. Use jewelry glue to attach your completed gem to the ring form.

Royal Rings

Gems from a stained glass store make eye-catching centerpieces on these rings that are fit for a queen! Adjustable ring forms found in the jewelry section of your local craft store will fit almost any finger, meaning you can share your regal creation with family and friends.

Tools and materials:

- ❑ Soldering tools and supplies (see page 39)
- ❑ Faceted flat-backed glass gem
- ❑ Scrapbook paper
- ❑ 5/16" (8mm)-wide black-backed wavy edged copper foil tape
- ❑ 1 copper foil tape sheet
- ❑ Jewelry glue
- ❑ Decoupage glue and brush
- ❑ Craft scissors
- ❑ 1 adjustable ring form
- ❑ Permanent marker or paint pen to color solder (optional)

The author used these products for the project. Substitute your choice of brands, tools, and materials as desired.

Suzann's Sensational Soldering Tip

Dress it down. If you would like to make a ring with a less formal look, replace the gem with a clear glass pebble from the floral department of your local craft store.

Filled with Hope Awareness Pin

Bring awareness and a little bling to the fight against breast cancer!

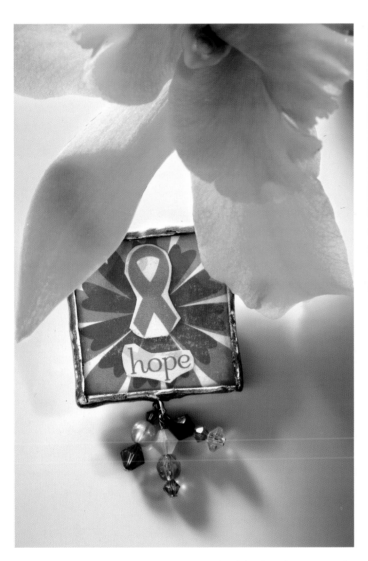

Tools and materials:

- ❏ Soldering tools and supplies (see page 39)
- ❏ Pin back
- ❏ Jewelry glue
- ❏ Decoupage glue and brush
- ❏ One 16- or 18-gauge jump ring
- ❏ Scrapbook paper
- ❏ Pink breast cancer awareness ribbon
- ❏ 1 "Hope" word
- ❏ Craft scissors
- ❏ 9 Swarovski crystals in various colors
- ❏ Three 2" (51mm)-long silver head pins
- ❏ Round-nose pliers
- ❏ Chain-nose pliers

The author used these products for the project. Substitute your choice of brands, tools, and materials as desired.

String three Swarovski crystals onto each of the head pins. Attach the head pins to the jump ring at the bottom of the pin by using your pliers to form a loop at the top of each head pin.

Fancy Face Floral Pin

Put a fresh face forward to the world with this vintage-style pin. I used a purchased, ready-made paper flower for this project, so it only took minutes to assemble.

Tools and materials:

- ❑ Soldering tools and supplies (see page 39)
- ❑ ⁵⁄₁₆" (8mm)-wide, wavy, black-backed copper foil tape
- ❑ 1 flat-backed glass stone
- ❑ Vintage clip art of female face
- ❑ Craft scissors
- ❑ 1 paper flower scrapbook embellishment with center removed
- ❑ 1 pin back
- ❑ Decoupage glue and brush
- ❑ Jewelry glue

The author used these products for the project. Substitute your choice of brands, tools, and materials as desired.

Brush decoupage glue on the petals of the paper flower to seal the paper. With this added protection, you'll be able to proudly wear your flower pin without risk of wear and tear.

Halloween Treat

Don't let this project scare you! Because this pendant has more than one use, it is a real treat. If you're hosting a ghoulish get together, make personalized favor bags for each guest by tying a custom soldered tag to each bag. When the party is over, the guests can turn the tags into pendants for necklaces as a way to remember the fabulous time they had. This technique works for any holiday event or special occasion.

Tools and materials:

- ❑ Soldering tools and supplies (see page 39)
- ❑ One 1" x 3" (25 x 76mm) piece of Halloween scrapbook paper
- ❑ Two 1" x 3" (25 x 75mm) glass microscope slides
- ❑ 9" (229mm) of 5⁄16" (8mm)-wide copper foil tape
- ❑ One 16- or 18-gauge jump ring
- ❑ Letters cut from various magazines to spell name
- ❑ Craft scissors
- ❑ Decoupage glue and brush
- ❑ Black paint pen to color solder (optional)

The author used these products for the project. Substitute your choice of brands, tools, and materials as desired.

Golden Glam Earrings

These sparkling gems will light up any room. They're easy to make and are the perfect gift for a friend or family member.

Tools and materials:

- ❏ Soldering tools and supplies (see page 39)
- ❏ 2 teardrop-shaped concave gems
- ❏ 2 pieces of scrapbook paper, cut to size
- ❏ 1 copper foil tape sheet, cut to size
- ❏ Edging scissors
- ❏ Craft scissors
- ❏ ½" (13mm)-wide copper foil tape
- ❏ 2 flat-backed Aurora Borealis Swarovski crystals
- ❏ 2 Aurora Borealis Swarovski rondelles
- ❏ 2 gold eye pins
- ❏ Two 16- or 18-gauge jump rings
- ❏ 1 pair of gold earring findings
- ❏ Jewelry glue
- ❏ Round-nose pliers
- ❏ Chain-nose pliers

The author used these products for the project. Substitute your choice of brands, tools, and materials as desired.

Trace the shape of your gems onto the scrapbook paper and the copper foil. Cut out the gem shapes. Glue one Swarovski crystal onto the center of each scrapbook paper cutout. Then, glue the scrapbook paper cutouts to the backs of the gems so that the Swarovski crystals are sitting inside of the concave section. Place the copper foil cutouts over the back of the scrapbook paper attached to the gems. Thread a Swarovski rondelle onto each eye pin and use your pliers to form a loop at the end of each eye pin. Using the eye pin loops, attach one end of an eye pin to the jump ring on the top of a concave gem. Attach the other end to an earring finding. Repeat with the remaining rondelle and concave gem to form the second earring.

(5)

Inspirational Ideas

As your soldering skills grow, you will feel that desire to branch out and start designing some soldered creations of your own. Sometimes developing a design concept can be the hardest part of making a project. Here are some finished projects to help inspire you and ignite the spark of ingenuity. You can incorporate countless materials into your soldering projects, so let your originality shine in each piece!

Beadphoria™(bēd'fôr'ē) *noun*
a feeling or state of intense excitement and
happiness when around beads and jewelry
making supplies: Creating joy one bead at a
time.™

Jewelry Journal

Project List
Soldering Iron
Ld. Free Solder
Floss
Foil

Hollywood Glamor

Memories of Oma

Des Colores Marisa

Blue Flower Pendant

Valentine Charms

Butterfly Pendant

Creepy Crawly Halloween

You Are So MOD

QR Code

This necklace design was the Craft and Hobby Association's 2011 Designer Press Kit winner.

Index

Acquisition editor: Peg Couch

Copy editors: Paul Hambke and Heather Stauffer

Cover and page designer: Lindsay Hess

Layout designer: Ashley Millhouse

Editor: Katie Weeber

Photography: Suzann Sladcik Wilson and William K. Sladcik

Proofreader: Lynda Jo Runkle

Indexer: Jay Kreider

More Great Books from Fox Chapel Publishing and Design Originals

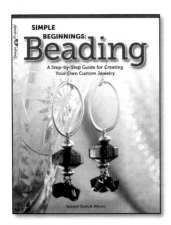

Simple Beginnings: Beading
ISBN 978-1-57421-415-4 **$14.99**
DO5386

**Easy & Elegant Beaded
Copper Jewelry**
ISBN 978-1-56523-514-4 **$24.95**

Bead-by-Bead
ISBN 978-1-57421-660-8 **$16.99**
DO5349

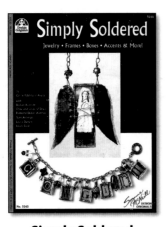

Simply Soldered
ISBN 978-1-57421-553-3 **$12.99**
DO5243

Jewelry Fixups
ISBN 978-1-56523-563-2 **$24.95**

Essential Links for Wire Jewelry
ISBN 978-1-57421-345-4 **$9.99**
DO3468

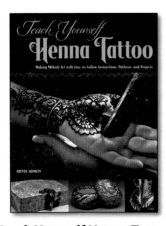

Teach Yourself Henna Tattoo
ISBN 978-1-57421-414-7 **$19.99**
DO5385

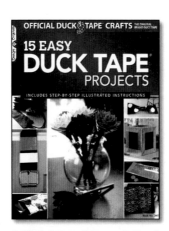

**Official Duck Tape® Craft
Book (Fox Edition)**
ISBN 978-1-57421-350-8 **$8.99**
DO3473

Steampunk Your Wardrobe
ISBN 978-1-57421-417-8 **$19.99**
DO5388

RUST and PATINA Style

Creating Fashionable Finishes with Reactive Metal Paints

Suzanne McNeill

With contributions by Cheryl and Megan Darrow

Design Originals

an Imprint of Fox Chapel Publishing
www.d-originals.com

Rust and Patina

When I see old copper roofs aged to that beautiful verdigris color, it inspires me to experiment with creating that same effect. Using metallic (nonreactive) acrylic paints and glazes or reactive metal paints and patina solution, it is possible to achieve overnight what Mother Nature takes decades to accomplish. I have experimented with these paints on every kind of surface and really enjoy watching the effects appear, almost like magic.

Those who enjoy working with statues, ornaments, bottles, and found objects will appreciate home décor projects. If you enjoy working with metal, you will find tips and projects guaranteed to please.

As a paper artist, mixed-media artist, altered artist, scrapbooker, or card maker, you will be amazed by the awesome papers you can fabricate. These can serve as background papers, mats, borders, and die cuts. In no time, you'll be creating altered books, book covers, and bookmarks that shine with the nostalgia of antiqued metal.

For lovers of fabric, check out the projects for canvas tote bags and silk scarves. Use the projects in this book for inspiration to experiment with both metallic acrylic paints and reactive metal paints.

Happy crafting,

Suzanne McNeill

Acknowledgments

I would like the thank the following individuals for their wonderful contributions to this book:

Cheryl Darrow. Cheryl is the creative genius and force behind TENseconds Studio, a company that is devoted to finding "cool tools for cool people." She is an avid collector of all things, from iron, to fabric, to leather, to typewriters, just waiting for the opportunity to use them in her designs. Cheryl is the author of *Metal Effects*, *Die Art One*, and *Die Art Two*.

Megan Darrow. Megan is also part of the TENseconds Studio team and loves developing new products. She and Cheryl create weekly YouTube videos to share their latest crafting products and ideas with the world. Visit *tensecondsstudio.com* to learn more.

Elitia Hart. Elitia is a metal crafter who specializes in metal sheet embossing. She worked almost exclusively with pewter sheeting until she became a certified TENseconds Studio instructor and began working with the company's colored metals. Visit *pewterart.ca* to learn more.

Trisha Conlon. Trisha is an avid crafter who enjoys scrapbooking, painting, altered art, and soldering. She teaches at The Crafty Scrapper, and also teaches and helps create videos for TENseconds Studio.

Terri Thomas. Terri is a crafter who attends classes at TENseconds Studio. She loves to create and learn new techniques.

REACTIVE METAL PAINTS & PATINA SOLUTION, VerDay Paint & Patina by TENseconds Studio, Cheryl Darrow and Megan Darrow, *tensecondsstudio.com*

ISBN 978-1-57421-377-5

McNeill, Suzanne.
  Rust and patina style / Suzanne McNeill.
    pages cm
  Includes index.
  Summary: " Create breathtaking art that shines with the nostalgia of antiqued metal. Metal paints and patina solution allow you to achieve overnight what nature took decades to accomplish. This book shows you how to transform almost any object or material with the "industrial chic" look of distressed metal. *Rust & Patina Style* offers dozens of projects for creating amazing paper crafts, jewelry, clothing, home décor, mixed media, and so much more. Reactive paints can be used on almost anything… on paper, cardstock, chipboard, cardboard, canvas, cloth, wood, metal, plastic, tile, or brick. They contain metal particles that develop an antique look of rust and/or verdigris when patina solution is applied. The authors instruct you in all the basics of working with rust and patina, including painting, creating textures, and sealing. They provide guidance on materials, supplies, and techniques"-- Provided by publisher.
  ISBN 978-1-57421-377-5 (pbk.)
  1. Painting. 2. Decoration and ornament. I. Title.
  TT385.M383 2014
  745.7'23--dc23
              2013026433

Contents

An Introduction to
Metallic Paints and Glazes

Rich Espresso

Worn Penny

Bronze

Shimmering Silver

Glorious Gold

Emperor's Gold

Splendid Gold

Dark Patina

Festive Green

Metallic acrylic paints and glazes, available in a variety of colors, can be used to add the look of metal or antiqued metal to any project. These products are great for quickly creating a metallic or aged metallic look.

Because most metallic acrylics contain ground pearlescent or mica particles to create the look of metal, the paints are nonreactive. This means the particles in the paint do not change colors to create a rust or patina effect when patina solution is applied.

The Basic Technique

Follow this basic technique to apply metallic paints and glazes to any surface you desire. Experiment with different color combinations as desired to create the exact look you want. Also try different methods of application for the second coat, including using a soft cloth, sponge, or dry brush to create different effects.

1 **Prepare the paint.** Choose a color of metallic paint and shake the bottle well so the pearlescent or mica particles are distributed evenly throughout the acrylic medium. It helps to place the bottle upside down for about an hour before use. Pour a small amount of paint into a container. If your paint comes in a wide-mouth jar, you can apply the paint directly from the jar.

2 **Apply the paint.** Use a bristle paintbrush to apply a coat of metallic paint to your desired surface. Brush a basecoat of paint onto the surface. Allow the paint to dry. Apply a second coat if needed.

3 **Apply the glaze.** Use a rough sea sponge or towel to dab metallic glaze, or another color of metallic paint, over the basecoat to create the aged look of rust or patina. If you are working on an item with raised surfaces, try applying the glaze with a dry brush, or apply it with a paintbrush and then wipe away the excess with a soft cloth. Allow the glaze to dry.

4 **Seal the piece.** Add a clear coat of polymer finish to seal your finished project.

Experiment with Color

Try using these different combinations of metallic paint and glaze colors to create a variety of effects.

Splendid Gold metallic   Glorious Gold metallic

NO PATINA. Real gold does not become oxidized over time, so there is no need to create a rust or patina finish on gold surfaces. Leave them sparkling like new!

PATINA WITH METALLIC PAINTS AND GLAZES. Other pure metals, such as brass, copper, and bronze, become oxidized over time, resulting in a rust or patina effect. Antique your projects using these metallic paint colors to replicate a patina-like finish.

Emperor's Gold metallic basecoat with Festive Green glaze   Rich Espresso metallic basecoat with Festive Green glaze   Bronze metallic basecoat with Dark Patina glaze

Worn Penny metallic basecoat with Dark Patina glaze   Shimmering Silver metallic basecoat with Black Pearl glaze   Black acrylic basecoat with Copper metallic glaze

Ivory acrylic basecoat with Dark Patina metallic glaze   Ivory acrylic basecoat with Festive Green metallic glaze

PATINA OVER IVORY. Sponge or wipe a metallic paint or glaze over an Ivory basecoat to replicate a patina-like finish.

Antiqued Silver Necklace

BY SUZANNE MCNEILL

SURFACE: Clay

INSTRUCTIONS: Use an epoxy resin clay to create a variety of beads for your necklace (see page 61 for information on creating clay beads). Paint the beads with Shimmering Silver metallic paint. Allow the paint to dry. Then, antique the surface of the beads by painting on a coat of Black Pearl metallic paint. Use a soft cloth to wipe away the excess black paint from the high areas of the beads so that it only remains in the recessed areas. Seal the beads with a polymer spray finish and string them onto the necklace of your choice.

Shiny Metallic Birdhouse

BY SUZANNE MCNEILL

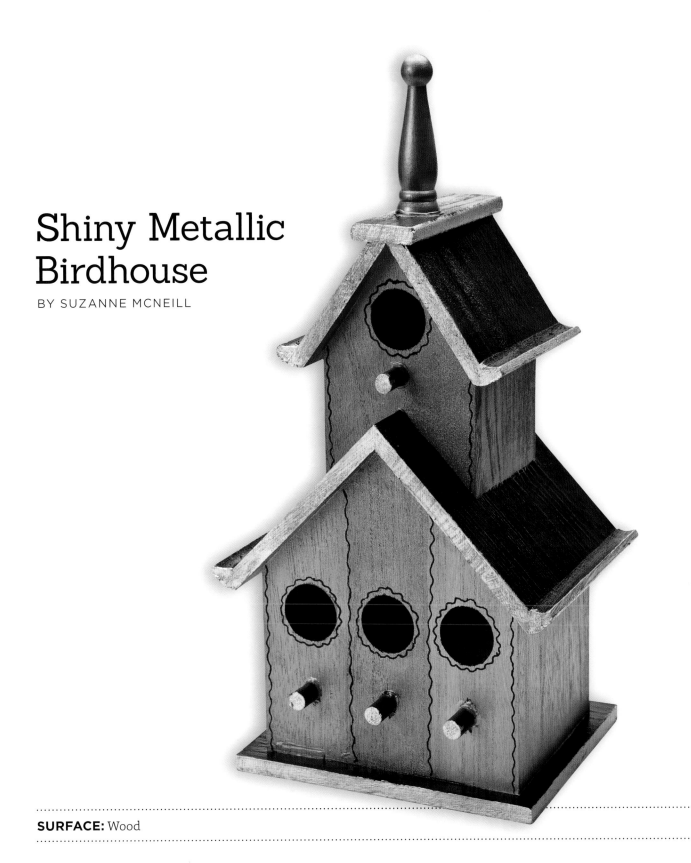

SURFACE: Wood

INSTRUCTIONS: Paint the front, sides, and spire of the birdhouse with metallic paints in Rich Espresso, Worn Penny, and Splendid Gold, creating the pattern or design of your choice. Antique the painted areas using additional coats of metallic paints or glazes, or leave them as they are, as shown. Paint the top of the roof and base with black acrylic paint. Paint the edges of the roof and base with Shimmering Silver. Paint the perches Black and the perch fronts Shimmering Silver. Add additional designs with a permanent marker once all the paint has dried.

An Introduction to
Reactive Metal Paints

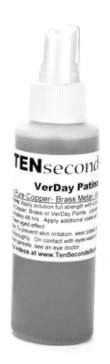

Reactive metal paints, available in colors such as Iron, Brass, Bronze, and Copper can be used on virtually any surface to create an aged rust or verdigris look.

Reactive metal paints—available in colors like Iron, Copper, Bronze, and Brass—and patina solution are special formulations. Genuine metal particles in the liquid paint react with the accompanying patina solution to create real rust and/or patina verdigris results. The Iron paint turns a rusty orange, while Brass, Bronze, and Copper paints acquire different shades of verdigris green.

Note: Reactive metal paints are different from metallic acrylic or other paints because the metal particles react with the patina solution. Acrylic paints that simply have a metallic color will not react with the patina solution and change color.

There are a variety of reactive metal paints available for purchase, and all the brands work in a similar manner. Personally, I love VerDay Paint & Patina by TENseconds Studio and used this brand

to create the projects in this book. I like the VerDay paints because they are formulated to give a vibrant and bold look. They are available in Brass, Copper, Bronze, and Iron colors. In addition, only one patina solution is needed to create a rust or patina reaction with any of the VerDay metal paints.

Reactive metal paints are incredibly versatile because they can be used on all types of surfaces, including paper, chipboard, cardboard, canvas, VerDay cloth, wood, plastic, clay, tile, brick, papier-mâché, ceramics, metal, and more. Basically, anything that can be painted with acrylic paint can be decorated with reactive metal paint and patina solution. The products work well on both rough and smooth surfaces. And no matter what the material, the technique for applying the paints and patina solution is basically the same.

The Basic Technique

Follow this basic technique to apply reactive metal paint and patina solution to any surface you desire. Create stunning rust and verdigris effects. Note that the patina solution works best if applied with a spray bottle.

Using reactive metal paint and patina solution is a creative process that cannot be rushed. Because it is a reactive process, the results will vary every time. The patina solution will normally begin to react with the metal in the paints about 20 minutes after application and is usually completely cured after 48 hours.

When you are finished, add highlights to your project by following Step 8 on page 12. To add more rust or verdigris color, paint sections with additional reactive metal paint. Spray patina solution on the painted sections. Allow the color to change and the paint and solution to dry overnight.

If you get more of the rust or verdigris color than you wanted, wait until the paint and patina dry completely and paint over the desired areas. You can repaint and reapply patina solution until you get the desired effect.

COLORS OF REACTIVE METAL PAINTS

IRON turns rusty orange
COPPER turns light green
BRASS turns green
BRONZE turns blue-green

Note: Iron has the strongest color and will overpower Copper if they are painted together.

Reactive metal paints can be applied to practically any surface. A patina spray is used to change the paint color to a rust or verdigris color. Here, Iron, Copper, Brass, and Bronze paint have been applied to paper. The patina solution was applied with a paintbrush to create the rust and patina letters.

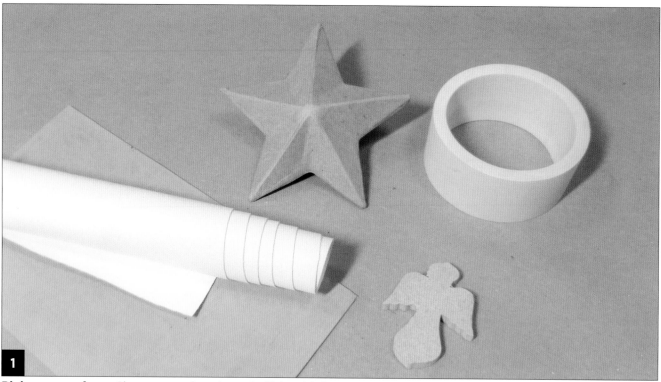

Pick your surface. Choose a surface to embellish—this basic technique can be used for paper, cardstock, canvas, VerDay cloth, clay, papier-mâché, ceramics, and more.

SUPPLIES

- Plastic gloves
- Paper to cover work surface (builder's paper or old newspapers)
- Bristle paintbrushes (one for each paint color)
- Small containers for paints
- Spray bottle for patina solution
- Rough sea sponge
- Paper towels

Prepare the paint. Choose a color of reactive metal paint and shake the bottle well so the metal particles are distributed evenly throughout the paint. It is important to shake the bottle before EACH use. Pour a small amount of the paint into a container (I like to use an old tuna fish can or a plastic dish).

Apply the paint.
Use a bristle paintbrush to apply a coat of the reactive metal paint to your desired surface. Allow the paint to dry (it will turn a dull color when dry, usually within an hour). Always allow the paint and patina solution to dry naturally. DO NOT use a heat gun or hair dryer to hasten the drying process.

Add a second coat. Apply a second coat of reactive metal paint. You can use the same color as the first coat or another color. Add a texture to this coat by making repeated small touches with the bristle brush for a stippled effect, or apply the paint with a small piece of rough sea sponge.

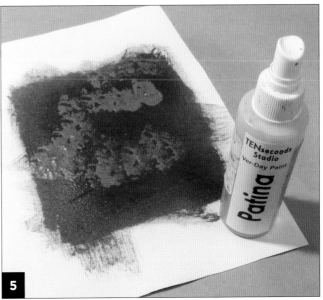

Spray on the patina solution. While the paint is still wet, apply the patina solution with a spray bottle. Apply the patina solution generously, letting it pool in recessed areas.

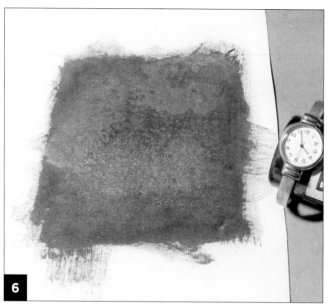

6 **Wait for the reaction.** Be patient. Allow the patina solution to react with the paint and dry. Dark brown/black Iron will change to rusty orange, and Brass, Bronze, and Copper will change to shades of blue-green verdigris. This reaction may begin as early as 20 minutes after application, or it may take a few hours before you start seeing a change.

7 **Check for the desired results.** Remember, be patient. The patina reaction and color change may take 24 to 48 hours. Look at the surface the next day and check the coloration. See if you want to alter any areas or whether you like the surface as it is. If desired, use a sea sponge to add more dark texture with paint. Allow it to dry.

Make any adjustments desired. To add highlights, paint sections with Brass, Bronze, and/or Copper. Spray patina solution on the painted sections. Allow the color to change and the paint and solution to dry overnight.

Seal the surface (optional). If desired, brush a coat of Mod Podge matte on the surface to seal it. Allow it to dry. You can also use clear spray acrylic sealer (it will darken the colors). This is especially important for items that will be worn or touched frequently, such as jewelry.

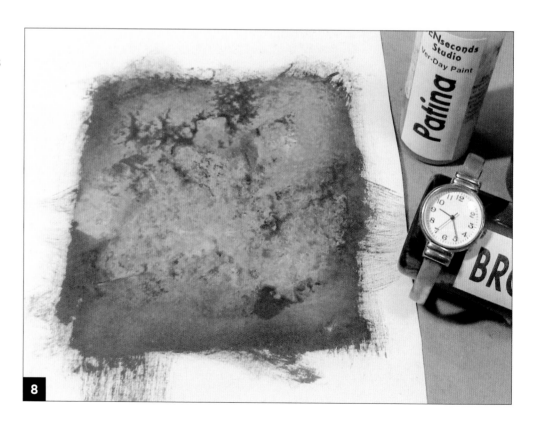

For use on metal sheeting

Pure metal sheeting and other metal pieces made of pure brass, copper, bronze, pewter, iron, and steel will react directly with the patina solution without the application of reactive metal paint. Before applying the patina solution, be sure the metal sheeting and/or pieces DO NOT have a protective lacquer finish, as this will not react with the patina solution. Use fine steel wool to rub any oil or dark coloration off of the metal's surface. Apply patina solution with a spray bottle or brush, and then wait a few hours for the reaction to change the color of the metal.

IMPORTANT: DO NOT use patina solution on an aluminum surface. It will not cause the color to change and may begin smoking (not a good thing). If you wish to use aluminum for a project, cover it with a primer first to prevent it from reacting badly with the patina. When using aluminum for a project, work in a well ventilated area and keep a protective mask on hand. If the aluminum reacts badly with the patina spray, make sure you open the windows and wear the mask until the fumes have dissipated.

Patina solution can be used to create rust and verdigris effects on pure metal sheeting and other pieces, such as Vintaj metal charms.

Selecting a sealer

Many of your finished items will need a coating of sealer to protect the surface—especially jewelry items or those that are going to be used frequently or outdoors. Be sure the item is totally dry before you seal it. I recommend brushing on a coating of Mod Podge with a matte finish. Clear spray acrylic sealer with a matte or satin finish also works well but tends to darken the colors.

Mod Podge matte and paint or spray-on acrylic sealers can all be used to finish rust and patina projects.

This paper shows the effects of various sealers on reactive metal paints. From the bottom left corner moving clockwise: no sealer, Mod Podge matte, clear Krylon spray sealer, and Minwax polyacrylic varnish were used.

Additional Techniques

Just like acrylic paint, reactive metal paint and patina can be used in a variety of ways and on a variety of surfaces to create the specific effect you want. Try some of these techniques to create different results on your projects.

Vary the paint application

Each reactive metal paint can be used alone. A solid area of Iron, Brass, Bronze, or Copper will have wonderful variations of color once the patina solution is applied. Iron turns a rusty orange in the patina areas. Brass, Bronze, and Copper turn wonderful variations of blue-green verdigris.

You can also apply VerDay metal paints side by side or overlay them. If you overlay them when wet, the paints get a bit muddy. If you let the first color dry for at least one hour, then sponge or stipple another color on top, you get an intriguing effect.

Note: Be aware that Iron is the strongest color and may overpower the other colors (especially Copper) when the patina solution is applied.

Paint on the patina solution

You can paint patina solution onto the reactive metal paint rather than spraying it on. This gives you the ability to create letters or shapes on a solid area of VerDay metal paint. I used a ½" (1.5cm) soft flat brush to paint letters with patina solution over dry reactive metal paint (see pages 9 and 27). (I poured a small amount of patina solution from the spray bottle into a plastic cup to use for painting.) As the solution dried, the letters I had painted appeared in their rust/verdigris colors.

If you use this technique, you may find that you need to make a few corrections. To strengthen the color of the letters, paint on additional patina solution. Then allow it to dry overnight. To cover any runs or drips in the background, paint over them with reactive metal paint in the original Iron, Brass, Bronze, or Copper.

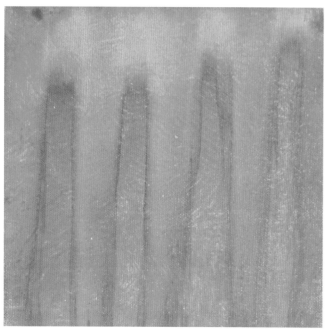

Try applying patina to a solid-color paint in a regular pattern. Here I've used Iron metal paint and created drips of rust with the patina solution.

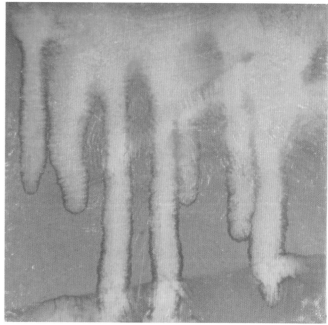

Apply more patina solution than you need. Then tilt your project, allowing the excess to roll over the surface and create irregular drips. This shows Iron metal paint with irregular drips of rust.

Add texture and patterns

There are a variety of ways to add texture to your projects. Try using a bristle brush to create a drybrush effect. Or stipple the paint with a bristle brush to make a rough texture. Use a stipple brush to give a different texture. Or apply reactive metal paint with a rough sea sponge or bubble wrap.

Create wonderful textures and patterns using rubber or foam stamps. Paint a surface with Brass metal paint and let it dry. Paint Iron metal paint onto a stamp. Immediately stamp the design onto the surface. Spray on patina solution and let it dry. See page 18 for more texturing ideas.

Use a spray application of patina solution for a random effect. Here, I sprayed patina solution over a puddle of Copper metal paint. Next, I tilted the surface in different directions to create drips all around the center puddle.

Use two different paint colors to get two different patina effects. This shows a combination of Iron and Bronze metal paint sprayed with patina solution.

Apply "sludge"

When rinsing reactive metal paint from brushes, save the dirty water. After you've rinsed a lot of brushes and set the water aside for a time, the metal particles from the paint will fall to the bottom of your water container to create a thick sediment or "sludge." This sludge can be used to dye scraps of paper or fabric for future projects. I call this "Money Water" because you don't need to purchase it. Brush the sludge over paper, cloth, or another surface to create a colorwash effect. Spray the area with patina solution and allow it to dry. Repeat the application for a darker coloration. Allow it to dry.

Rinse your brushes in a container so you can save the water. Use the sediment or "sludge" of metal particles that settles at the bottom as reative metal paint to paint on future projects.

Sludge from dirty water applied to paper and sprayed with patina solution.

Experiment on paper

If you are using reactive metal paints for the first time, experimenting on paper is perfect for learning what to expect from them. Paper is inexpensive, has many uses, and allows you to see the reactions of the metal paint and patina solution easily. Use paper to practice some of the techniques listed previously. Save your experimental paper for future projects.

BUILDER'S PAPER. If you haven't discovered the joys of crafting with contractor's or builder's paper, you are in for a pleasant surprise. Builder's paper (tan colored paper used by painters to protect surfaces from drips) is one of my favorite papers and makes a great rustic surface for rust and verdigris effects. Builder's paper comes in a large roll and is inexpensive and sturdy. It can be found at hardware stores and large home repair stores. Cardstock and chipboard are also great surfaces.

HELPFUL HINTS

- Shake each bottle of reactive metal paint well before EACH use to suspend the metal particles in the emulsion and prevent them from settling to the bottom of the bottle.
- The patina solution reacts best with wet paint when it is sprayed onto the surface. However, patina solution can also be applied to dry paint. It can be sprayed on, applied with a bristle or foam brush, or dabbed on with a rough sea sponge. Each type of application will yield a different look.
- The drying/curing process works best in a warm location. Place small projects in the sun or on a sunny windowsill to activate the patina solution and speed up the process. Note: A heat gun or hair dryer does not help. DO NOT try to hasten the process with these tools.
- When you have excess reactive metal paint on a surface, place a piece of paper over it and press. When you pull the items apart you will have two unique surfaces to use in your projects. You can also remove the excess with a stipple brush and apply it onto another project.

While you're experimenting, try these three different methods of adding texture to the paper:

TEXTURE WITH BUBBLE WRAP. Apply reactive metal paint to paper. Let it dry. Apply reactive metal paint to the raised bubbles on a piece of bubble wrap with a brush. Press the bubbles onto the painted paper to add texture. While wet, spray patina solution on the surface. Let it dry.

TEXTURE WITH PLASTIC WRAP. Paint paper with one color of reactive metal paint. Let it dry. Sponge on more reactive metal paint in random areas. While wet, spray patina solution on the surface. Cover the paper with plastic wrap and let it dry overnight.

MULTI-COLOR SURFACES. Paint colors of reactive metal paint side by side on a surface for a rustic effect.

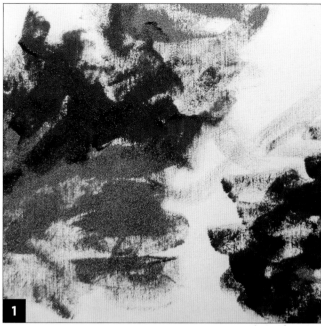

1

Apply the first coat. Try applying the reactive metal paint on paper with a bristle brush. Experiment with different types of papers to see the different effects you can create just by changing the surface. Try applying different colors of reactive metal paint side by side on a page.

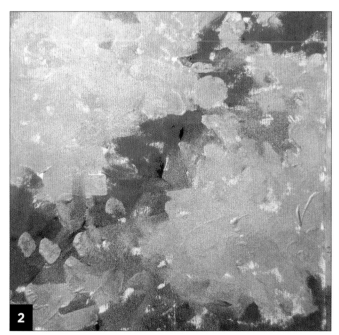

2

Apply additional coats. Apply more reactive metal paint or a different color of reactive metal paint to create blotches and textures. You can add this second coat of paint over your first coat or on unpainted areas of the paper. Experiment by applying the reactive metal paint with different applicators, such as bubble wrap, a sea sponge, a dry bristle brush, etc.

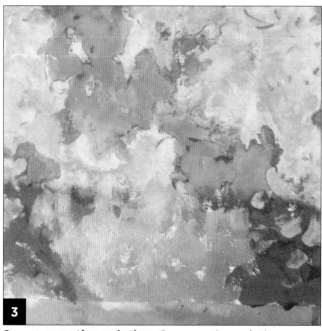

3

Spray on patina solution. Spray patina solution on various areas of the paper in a random manner. Let it dry overnight.

Creating Texture

Textures invite the hand and draw the eye to any piece of art. The more variety you have in the texture of a piece, the more interesting it will be. Using unexpected materials to create texture will yield uniquely pleasing results.

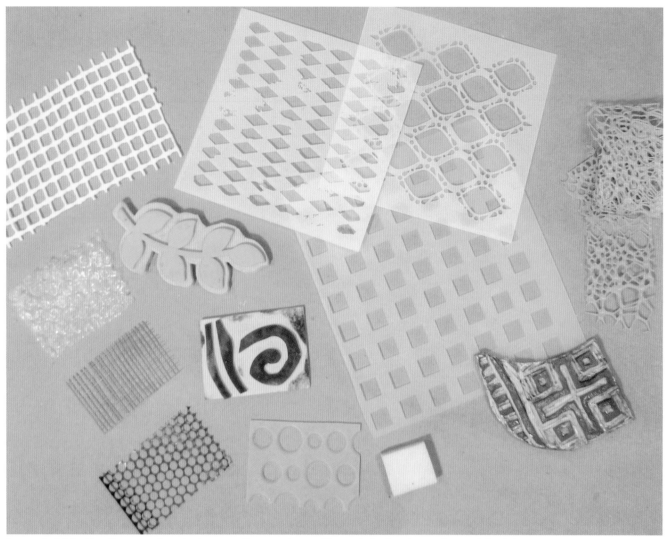

Any material that has its own unique texture or pattern can be used to create texture in reactive metal paint, including stamps, stencils, sponges, bubble wrap, and punchinella ribbon.

TOOLS FOR TEXTURING: Bubble wrap, sea sponges, dry bristle paintbrushes, rug canvas, and foam brushes are just a few items that create wonderful textures. Experiment with these on scrap paper, and then use your favorites for additional projects.

Apply paint to your project. Then, apply the second coat of paint using the texturing tool of your choice, or first apply the paint and then use the texturing tool to apply the patina solution. Each type of application will yield a different look. Remember, the patina solution reacts best with wet paint.

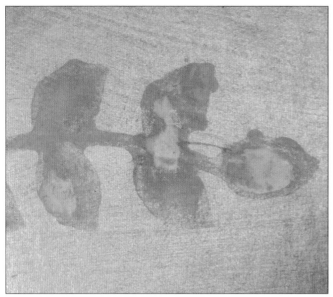

Patina solution applied with foam stamp

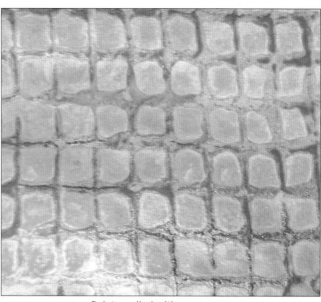

Paint applied with rug canvas

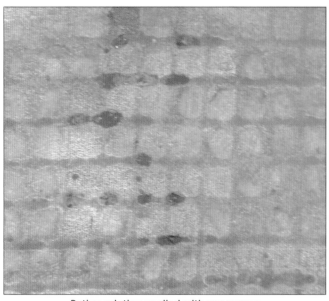

Patina solution applied with rug canvas

Paint textured with brushstrokes

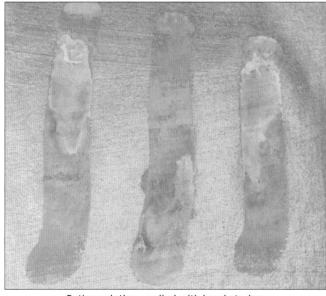

Patina solution applied with brushstrokes

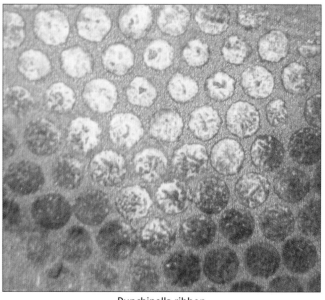

Punchinella ribbon

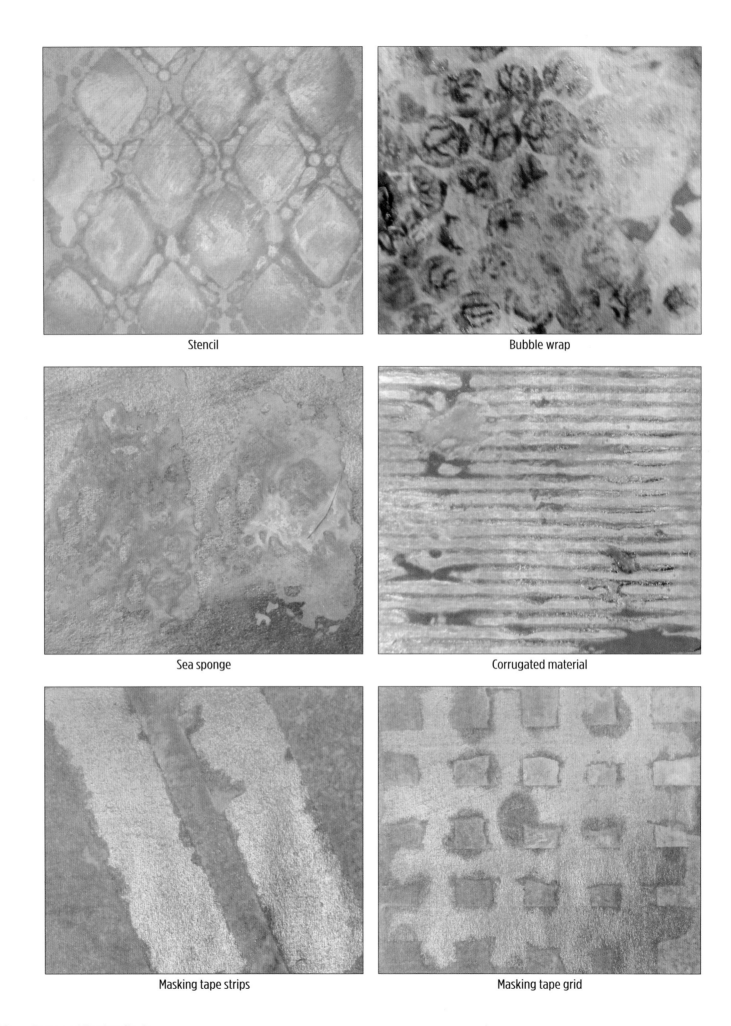

Stencil

Bubble wrap

Sea sponge

Corrugated material

Masking tape strips

Masking tape grid

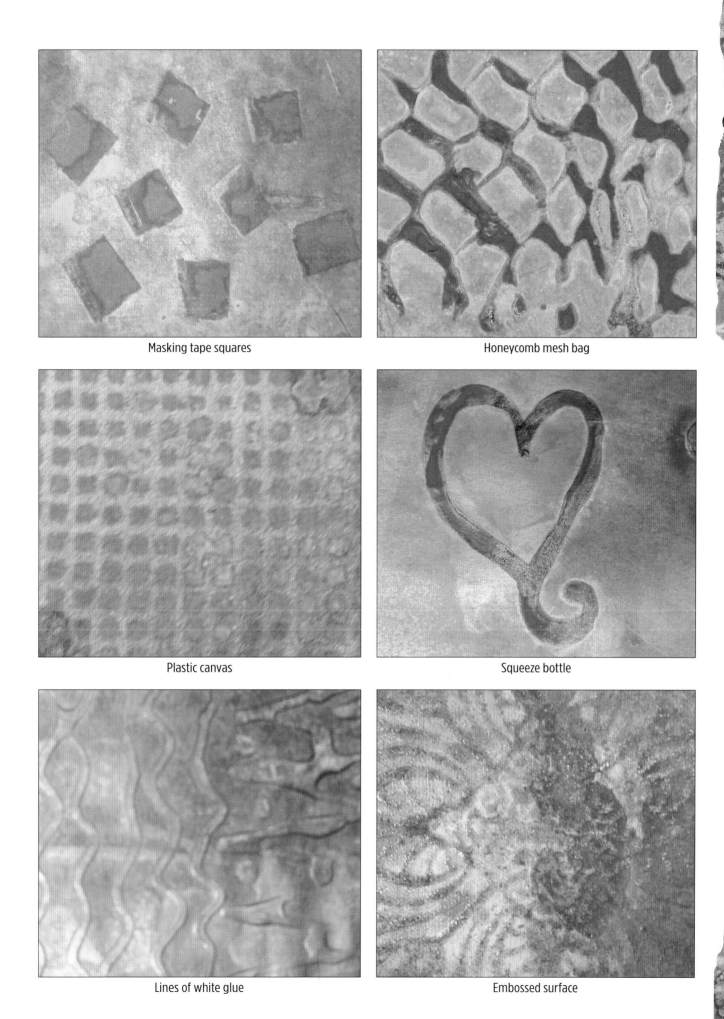

Masking tape squares

Honeycomb mesh bag

Plastic canvas

Squeeze bottle

Lines of white glue

Embossed surface

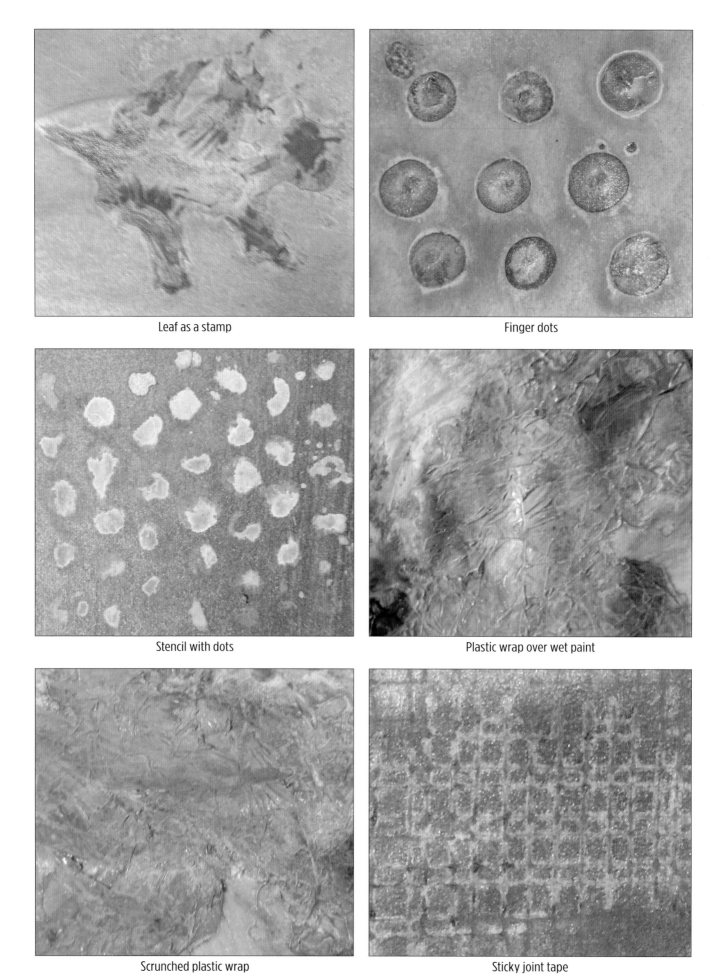

Leaf as a stamp

Finger dots

Stencil with dots

Plastic wrap over wet paint

Scrunched plastic wrap

Sticky joint tape

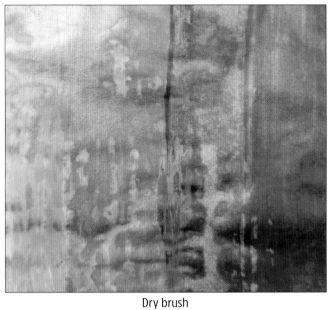

Dry brush

Drips of paint

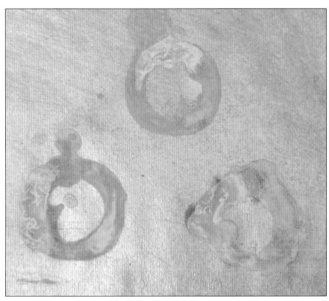

Medicine bottle stamps

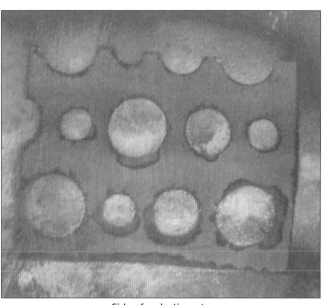

Side of a plastic crate

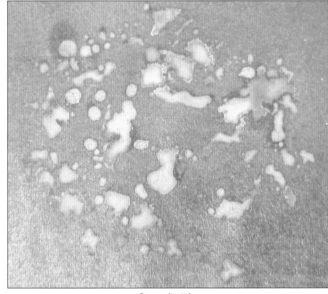

Spray bottle

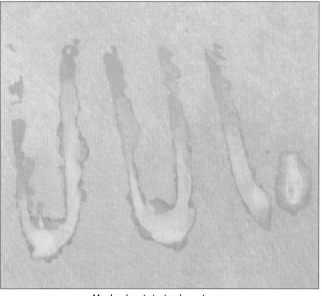

Mashed potato tool as stamp

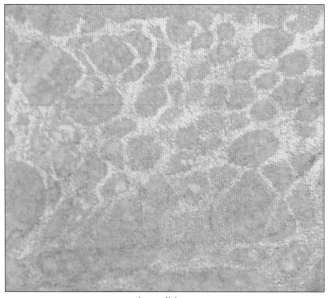

Lacy ribbon

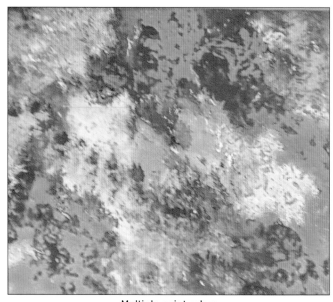

Multiple paint colors

"Sludge" from dirty paintbrush water

GET CREATIVE!

Reactive metal paints and patina solution can truly be used for any project. Check out some of the related projects, like the Aged Book on page 28, the Mixed-Media Booklet on page 78, and the Rust and Patina Journal on page 84. Then, see if you can use those projects to create a journal like this one that you can fill with your art and thoughts!

Projects

Reactive metal paints and patina solution can be used on countless surfaces to create truly unique effects. The following pages are filled with more than fifty projects to get you started and ignite your creativity. Use these projects to inspire your own rust and patina creations, made to fit your taste and style.

Accordion-Fold Booklet

BY CHERYL DARROW

SURFACE: Paper

Give yourself an introduction to working with reactive metal paints and patina by creating this little booklet. It's super-simple to put together and makes a great card or decoration.

INSTRUCTIONS: Start with a rectangle of painted paper that is about 9" x 12" (23 x 30.5cm). Fold it in half lengthwise. Fold the double layer in half crosswise. Fold the outer flaps back toward the center fold to form an accordion with four equal sections. Turn the folded piece so the end flaps are facing toward you.

Glue small embellishments and images to the paper. Write words and details on the pages with black and white colored pencils. Tie a ribbon around one of the folds.

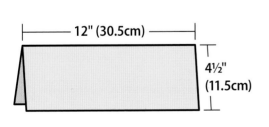

12" (30.5cm)

4½" (11.5cm)

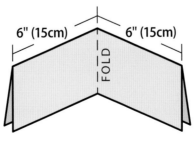

6" (15cm) 6" (15cm)

FOLD

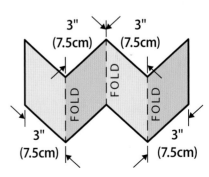

3" (7.5cm) 3" (7.5cm)

FOLD FOLD FOLD

3" (7.5cm) 3" (7.5cm)

Lampshade

BY TERRI THOMAS

SURFACE: Paper

Complement a lamp by applying reactive metal paint and patina to a paper lampshade for an elegant effect.

YOU'LL NEED: A paper lampshade, bristle paintbrush, sponge, plastic wrap, reactive metal paints, and patina solution.

INSTRUCTIONS: Paint the lampshade with Copper metal paint. Let it dry. Sponge Copper, Bronze, and Iron metal paint in random areas. While wet, spray patina solution on the lampshade. Cover the lampshade with plastic wrap and let it dry overnight.

Entryway Wall

BY MEGAN DARROW

SURFACE: Entryway wall

Absolutely breathtaking! This is the wall in the entryway of a home. It feels very welcoming, leaving you with the expectation that what comes next will be equally inviting and elegant. Iron metal paint and patina solution created this million-dollar look on a renovation budget. Best of all, this is a weekend project that will actually be *finished* at the end of the weekend!

YOU'LL NEED: Dark primer paint, roller applicator, paintbrush, sealer of your choice, reactive metal paints, and patina solution.

INSTRUCTIONS: Paint the wall with the darkest primer paint available. Let the primer dry overnight. Brush Iron metal paint onto the wall. Let it dry overnight. Apply a second coat of Iron paint. Spray the wall with patina solution to make drips and change the paint color as desired. Let the wall dry overnight. Seal the wall.

Calligraphy Papers

BY CHERYL DARROW

SURFACE: Paper

Create posh papers for cards, booklets, invitations, and notecards by using patina solution to create lettering in rust and verdigris colors.

IMAGINE: Cover paper with Bronze metal paint. Allow it to dry. Use a soft ¼" (0.5cm) flat brush to apply patina solution, painting marks, dots, letters, and/or words onto the paper. Allow the color to change and the solution to dry. Repeat if needed.

SCRIBBLES AND DOODLES: Cover paper with Copper metal paint. Allow it to dry. Put a small amount of Iron metal paint in a squeeze bottle. Apply the Iron paint to the paper with the bottle. While the paint is still wet, spray enough patina solution onto the paper to make a puddle. Tilt the paper left, right, up, and down, allowing dribbles of paint to roll across the paper. Allow the color to change and the solution to dry.

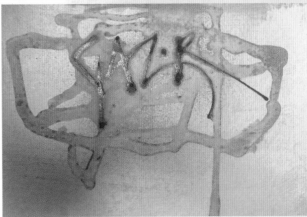

FREEDOM AND ALPHABET: Cover paper with Brass metal paint. Allow it to dry. Put a small amount of Iron metal paint in a squeeze bottle. Apply the Iron paint to the paper with the bottle. While wet, spray patina solution onto the paper. Allow the color to change and the solution to dry.

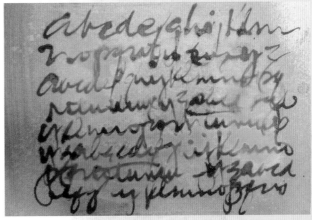

Aged Book

BY CHERYL DARROW

SURFACE: Paper

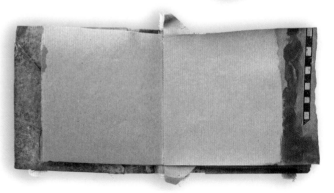

It's great to use surfaces that are recycled, and this project fits that perfectly. Whenever you work with reactive metal paint, it can be good to have a piece of tan paper on the table to protect the surface. This book uses that paper. That's right...for this project, the cover was made from dirty tan paper! The paper already contained marks and paint splatters made during previous paintings. You can add some more marks, sponge on paint, and then spray the entire piece with patina solution. The inside cover has a folded pocket with stitched edging—just right for tucking in notes and photos. The pages are embellished with rubber stamp images, ink drawings, and a collage.

YOU'LL NEED: Cardstock or builder's paper, strip of canvas, strong thread (buttonhole, carpet, or waxed linen), #24 needle, sewing machine, embellishments as desired, paintbrush, reactive metal paints, and patina solution.

FOR THE COVER: Cut one 15½" x 22" (39.5 x 56cm) piece of tan cardstock or builder's paper and decorate it as desired using reactive metal paints and patina solution. Fold the left and right ends toward the center, creating two flaps each 5½" (14cm). Leaving the ends folded in, fold the top and bottom edges toward the center, creating two flaps each 5" (12.5cm).

FOR THE COVER POCKET: Fold the cover down the vertical center. Open the center fold of the cover. Using the center fold as a reference, cut a slit down the center of the bottom flap (cut only the outside of the bottom flap). Fold each side of the bottom flap at a diagonal to form a pocket on each side of the inside of the cover. Tuck the top flap into the diagonal pockets.

FOR THE PAGES: Cut two 5" x 10½" (12.5 x 26.5cm) pieces, two 4½" x 10" (11.5 x 25.5cm) pieces, and two 4½" x 4½" (11.5 x 11.5cm) pieces of tan cardstock or builder's paper. Decorate the pages as desired using reactive metal paints and patina solution. Embellish as desired with rubber stamp images, rub-ons, or collage elements.

FOR THE COVER STITCHING: Using a sewing machine, stitch around the edges of the folded cover, adding decorative stitches if desired. Zigzag stitch a canvas strip along the edge of the cover to add texture.

TO FINISH THE BOOK: Stack each set of pages together. Center the largest set of pages on the cover. Repeat with the next largest set of pages. Center the square set of pages on point on top of the other pages to form a diamond shape. Stitch down the center of the book to attach the pages to the cover.

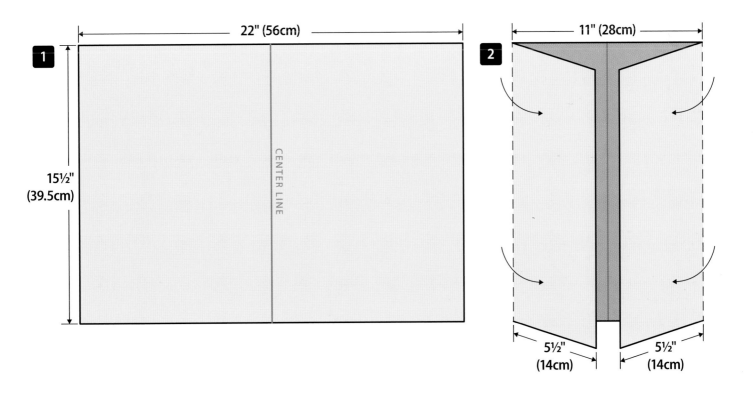

3

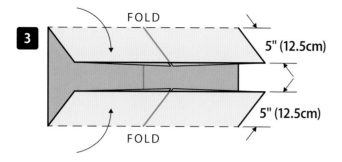

FOLD

5" (12.5cm)

5" (12.5cm)

FOLD

4

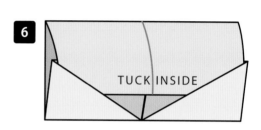

CUT THE OUTSIDE FLAP

5

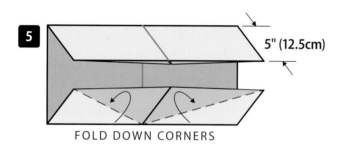

5" (12.5cm)

FOLD DOWN CORNERS

6

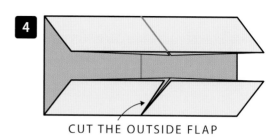

TUCK INSIDE

7

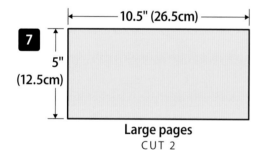

10.5" (26.5cm)

5"
(12.5cm)

Large pages
CUT 2

8

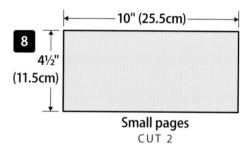

10" (25.5cm)

4½"
(11.5cm)

Small pages
CUT 2

9

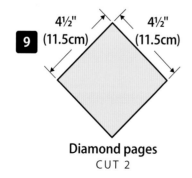

4½"
(11.5cm)

4½"
(11.5cm)

Diamond pages
CUT 2

10

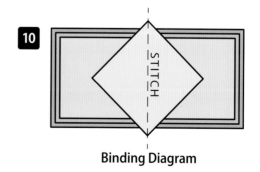

STITCH

Binding Diagram

Sleeping Cherub Figurine

BY CHERYL DARROW

SURFACE: Plaster

Angels are such a popular motif that Cheryl just had to make one, and this plaster cherub was too cute to pass up.

YOU'LL NEED: A plaster angel statue, paintbrush, reactive metal paints, and patina solution.

INSTRUCTIONS: Paint the wings of the angel with Bronze metal paint and the body with Iron. Let it dry. Apply more Iron paint to the body and more Bronze to the wings. Spray the statue with patina solution. Let it dry. Repeat until you achieve the desired effect.

I Dream of Jeannie Bottle

BY CHERYL DARROW

SURFACE: Ceramic

Thrifty décor: this ceramic piece was a great thrift store find, but it was a really ugly red. No worries. Cheryl altered it to suit her upscale taste, and it was really easy.

YOU'LL NEED: A carved or textured item, sandpaper, clear spray sealer, paintbrush, sea sponge, reactive metal paints, and patina solution.

INSTRUCTIONS: Start by roughing up the surface with sandpaper. Apply Copper metal paint to the surface. Allow it to dry. Use a sea sponge to apply more Copper to various areas of the surface as desired. Spray with patina solution. Allow the patina solution to dry overnight and the paint to change color. Repeat until you get the desired effect. Apply spray sealer to finish the piece.

This piece started out as an unattractive red color. A quick application of reactive metal paints and patina solution easily transformed it into a beautiful piece of décor.

Love Sizzles Canvas

BY SUZANNE MCNEILL

SURFACE: Stretched canvas, papier-mâché

Hearts afire! This wall décor deserves to be displayed in a gallery or in your home. Make it yourself. Make it gorgeous. Make it today.

Papier-mâché is light, inexpensive, widely available, and comes in every shape, size, and motif you could desire. It's a treasure trove for artists seeking new and interesting canvas and makes a perfect centerpiece for this project.

YOU'LL NEED: A 12" x 12" (30.5 x 30.5cm) stretched canvas, an 8" x 8" (20.5 x 20.5cm) papier-mâché heart with a flat back, molding paste, frame hanger, extra-strong all-purpose glue (I recommend Goop glue), palette knife, paintbrush, sludge, reactive metal paints, and patina solution.

1 Use the palette knife to apply a 2" (5cm)-wide border of rough molding paste around the canvas square. Use the palette knife to apply a 2" (5cm)-wide strip of molding paste with lines on the front of the heart. Allow the paste to dry overnight.

2 Paint the canvas, including the molding paste, with sludge (see page 15). Paint the inner square and edges of the canvas with Iron metal paint. Apply Copper metal paint to the top outer edges of the heart. Apply Iron metal paint to the molding paste on the heart and the heart's outside edges. Apply Brass metal paint in the center of the heart. Allow it to dry. Add a second coat of paint to each area.

3 Spray patina solution over the canvas and heart. Allow it to dry overnight. Add more paint and patina solution in areas as desired.

4 Glue the canvas and heart together. Set a book or heavy object on top of the heart so it will dry flat against the canvas. Attach the frame hanger after everything has dried.

Greeting Cards with Wood Accents

BY SUZANNE MCNEILL

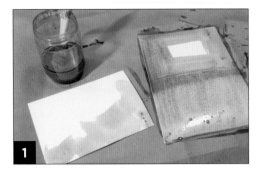

SURFACE: Paper, wood

Special distressed coloring makes these cards unique. Transform the paper and wood with touches of rust and patina.

YOU'LL NEED: A 4¼" x 11" (11.5 x 28cm) piece of cream cardstock, a 3" to 4" (7.5 to 10cm) wood cutout, glue (I recommend Elmer's Glue-All), paintbrush, sludge, reactive metal paints, and patina solution.

1 Fold the cardstock to 4¼" x 5½" (11.5 x 14cm). Paint the cardstock with sludge (see page 15). Spray patina solution onto the surface. Allow it to dry.

2 Paint the wood cutout with Copper or Iron metal paint. Allow it to dry. Add a second coat of Copper or Iron. Spray patina solution onto the surface. Allow it to dry.

3 Glue the wood accent onto the cardstock. Allow the glue to dry overnight.

Serenity Mask Canvas

BY SUZANNE MCNEILL

SURFACE: Stretched canvas, plastic

"Legacy, Memory, Expression, Identity..." Create the feeling of your inner self by adding cutout magazine words to a canvas. You can make it yourself today.

YOU'LL NEED: An 8" x 10" (20.5 x 25.5cm) stretched canvas, a 3" x 5" (7.5 x 12.5cm) plastic mask, molding paste, frame hanger, glue (I recommend Goop or Fabrico glue), Mod Podge matte, paintbrush, sea sponge, cutout words, reactive metal paints, and patina solution.

TO BEGIN: Assemble the pieces. Glue the mask to the canvas. Set a book or heavy object on top of the mask so it will dry flat against the canvas. Let the glue dry overnight. Apply molding paste around the edges of the mask to seal any openings. Apply a thin layer of molding paste to the top of the canvas on the left side. Let the paste dry overnight.

FOR THE MASK: Paint the mask with Brass metal paint. Spray patina solution over the mask. Allow it to dry overnight. Add more paint and patina solution in areas as desired.

TO FINISH: Paint the canvas with Iron metal paint on one side and Bronze metal paint on the other side. Allow the paint to dry. Use a sea sponge to apply more Bronze in selected areas on the Bronze side of the canvas. Spray patina solution over the canvas. Allow it to dry overnight. Add more paint and patina solution in areas as desired. Adhere cutout words to the canvas with Mod Podge matte as desired. Attach the frame hanger after everything has dried.

Tick Tock Antiqued Clock

BY SUZANNE MCNEILL

SURFACE: Plastic

Is it time for art yet? Of course! It's always art time at my house. I used an inexpensive plastic clock and painted the outer rim with reactive metal paints. Now it has an industrial chic look.

YOU'LL NEED: A plastic clock, screwdriver, paintbrush, sandpaper, clear spray sealer, reactive metal paints, and patina solution.

PREPARE THE CLOCK: Use a screwdriver to remove the small screws on the back of the clock. Separate the outside rim from the clock face and inner parts. Be sure to save all the pieces. Rough up the plastic surface of the clock's rim with sandpaper so the paint will better adhere to the surface.

PAINT THE CLOCK: Paint the outer edge of the clock rim with Iron metal paint, and paint the inner edge with Copper. Spray patina solution over the clock rim. Allow it to dry overnight. Add more paint and patina solution in areas as desired. Apply clear spray sealer.

ASSEMBLE THE CLOCK: Once the rim is dry, reassemble the clock by putting the clock rim, face, and inner parts back together. Add the screws.

Pretty Kitty Statuette

BY ELITIA HART

SURFACE: Ceramic, copper sheeting

Cheryl's daughter Megan received this statue for her birthday this year. She loves it. This purr-fectly gorgeous statue is everyone's favorite. It began as a white ceramic cat and was transformed with reactive metal paints and metal sheeting.

YOU'LL NEED: A ceramic statue, sandpaper, steel wool, thin pure copper sheeting, flower texture plate, texture tool, paintbrush, scissors for metal, a sheet of extra-strength double-sided adhesive (I recommend any brand with a pink color. There are many double-sided adhesive products on the market, and all claim to be strong. Ones with a pink color, though, are by far the strongest.), spray-on primer, molding paste, clear spray sealer, sea sponge, reactive metal paints, and patina solution.

TO BEGIN: Rough up the surface of the ceramic statue with sandpaper. Spray it with primer, and let it dry.

FOR THE CERAMIC STATUE: Paint the surface with Bronze metal paint. Allow it to dry. Use a sea sponge to apply more Bronze and a bit of Iron to areas of the surface. Spray it with patina solution. Allow it to dry overnight and the paint to change color.

FOR THE METAL FLOWERS: Clean the surface of the copper sheeting by rubbing it with steel wool. Place the sheeting over a flower texture plate. Rub the texture tool over the sheeting on the texture plate to emboss the designs onto the metal. Fill the back of the flower leaves in the sheeting with molding paste. Allow it to dry. Sponge the front of the flower leaves with patina solution. Allow it to dry. Attach the double-sided adhesive sheet to the back of the copper sheeting. Carefully cut out the flower and leaf shapes.

TO FINISH: Adhere the flowers and leaves to the ceramic statue. Apply spray sealer to finish the project.

Time in a Bottle Memorabilia Glass

BY TRISHA CONLON

....

SURFACE: Clay, paper

....

Reminiscent of a ship in a bottle, this project features many ideas that can be implemented alone or in combination.

YOU'LL NEED: A glass goblet, cloth, air-dry clay, glass knob, small photo, pleated paper rosette, silk flower, ribbon, glue (I recommend Fabri-Tac permanent adhesive), paintbrush, sea sponge, reactive metal paints, and patina solution.

INSTRUCTIONS: Wrap the stem end of the goblet with a cloth. Snap off the stem of the glass. The cloth will protect your fingers from any glass shards or splinters. Also be sure to wear goggles or another form of protection for your eyes. This can also be done with a hammer. Discard any shards of glass in a safe manner.

Turn the goblet upside down. This will form the bottom of your "bottle." Use the clay to make a bottle neck extending up from the goblet bottom. Allow the clay to dry. Paint the clay with Iron and Brass metal paints. Allow it to dry. Use a sea sponge to apply more Iron and Brass in selected areas. Spray patina solution over the clay. Allow it to dry overnight. Add more paint and patina solution in areas as desired. Add a glass knob to the top of the clay to look like a bottle stopper. Add a silk flower and ribbon at the top of the bottle neck.

For the inside of the bottle, apply reactive metal paint and patina solution to the pleated paper rosette. Place the rosette and photo inside the goblet. Add any additional embellishments as desired.

Canvas Art Collection

BY SUZANNE MCNEILL

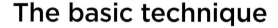

SURFACE: Stretched canvas, papier-mâché, paper

Experimenting with different kinds of media, mixing them up in new ways, and seeing what happens is fun. Dress up simple canvas hangings with dimensional items.

YOU'LL NEED: A 12" x 12" (30.5 x 30.5cm) stretched canvas, an 8" x 8" (20.5 x 20.5cm) canvas panel, a decorative item, glue (I recommend Goop or Fabrico glue), paintbrush, reactive metal paints, and patina solution.

The basic technique

1 Paint the stretched canvas and canvas panel with reactive metal paint as desired. I like to use the paint to create borders for my canvases.

2 If desired, paint a second color of reactive metal paint on the canvas pieces. I added an inner square on the large canvas. Then, paint your decorative item. My decorative star was originally a three-dimensional piece. I carefully cut along the edges with a craft knife to cut it in half so it would have a flat back.

3 Spray patina solution over everything. Allow it to dry overnight.

4 Layer the canvases and decorative items as desired. Then, glue everything together. Set a book on top of the assembly so everything will dry flat. Let the glue dry overnight.

SMALL ANGEL: Paint the large canvas with Iron. Paint the small canvas panel with Copper. Add a 6" (15cm) papier-mâché angel painted with Brass and Iron.

HEART IN A DIAMOND: Paint the large canvas with Copper. Paint the small canvas panel Iron. Attach it on point to the large canvas. Add a 6" (15cm) papier-mâché heart painted with Bronze.

STAR IN A SQUARE: Paint a border along the outer edges of the large canvas with Iron. Paint an inner border with Bronze. Paint the small canvas panel with Iron. Paint a 6" (15cm) papier-mâché star with Copper. Attach the star to the canvas.

HEART IN A SQUARE: Paint the large canvas with three colors: Copper to form an outer border, Brass to form an inner border, and Iron for the center. Add an 8" (20.5cm) papier-mâché heart painted with Copper. This piece does not include a small canvas panel.

BIRD: Paint the large canvas with Bronze. Paint the small canvas panel with Brass. Add a 6" (15cm) bird torn from 140# watercolor paper and painted with Iron.

CIRCLES: Paint a 10" (25.5cm)-diameter Bronze circle in the center of the large canvas. Paint the remainder of the canvas Iron. Tear 8", 6", 4" and 2" (20.5, 15, 10, and 5cm)-diameter circles from 140# watercolor paper. Paint the circles with Bronze, Iron, or Brass, and attach them to the canvas, working from largest to smallest.

VERTICAL STRIPES: Paint the large canvas with Brass. Paint the small canvas panel with Iron. Tear a 6" x 6" and a 4" x 6" (15 x 15 and 10 x 15cm) strip from 140# watercolor paper. Cut a 2" x 6" (5 x 15cm) strip from a piece of plastic with holes in it (I cut a piece from the side of a plastic crate). Paint the paper and plastic pieces with Iron, Copper, and Bronze. Adhere the pieces of watercolor paper and plastic to the small canvas panel in layers.

LARGE ANGEL: Paint the large canvas with Iron. Paint a small 6" x 6" (15 x 15cm) canvas panel with Iron. Do not add patina solution to the small canvas panel. Tear an 8" (20.5cm) angel and 8" (20.5cm) wings from 140# watercolor paper. Paint them with Copper and attach them to the canvas.

HOLES IN CHEESE: Paint the large canvas with Iron and Copper. Paint a small 6" x 6" (15 x 15cm) canvas panel with Brass. Paint a 5" (12.5cm)-diameter metal can lid with Copper. Paint a piece of 6" x 6" (15 x 15cm) plastic with holes in it with Iron (I cut the side off of a plastic crate). Attach the canvas panel on point, the can lid, and plastic to the large canvas.

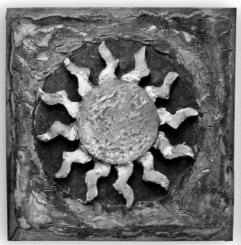

CIRCLES IN A DIAMOND: Paint the large canvas with Iron. Paint the small canvas panel with Copper. Paint a 6" (15cm)-diameter wood circle with Iron and a 4" (10cm)-diameter metal can lid with Iron. Attach the circles to the canvas.

SUNSHINE: Paint a 10" (25.5cm)-diameter circle in the center of the canvas with Iron. Paint a 1" border around the edges of the canvas with Iron. Paint the remainder of the canvas with Copper. Take an 8" (20.5cm) wood sun, and paint the center Bronze and the rays Iron. Attach the sun to the canvas.

HORIZONTAL STRIPES: Paint the canvas with Iron. Tear a 6" x 6", 4" x 6", and 3" x 6" (15 x 15, 10 x 15, and 7.5 x 15cm) strip from 140# watercolor paper. Also tear five 1" (1.5cm)-diameter circles from the paper. Paint the pieces of watercolor paper with Brass, Copper, Iron, and Bronze. Adhere pieces of watercolor paper to the canvas in layers.

STAR IN A DIAMOND: Paint the large canvas with Iron. Paint the small canvas panel with Copper. Add a 6" (15cm) papier-mâché star painted with Iron.

HEART IN A HEART: Paint a heart in the center of the canvas with Iron. Paint outside the heart with Iron and inside the heart with Copper. Add a 6" (15cm) papier-mâché heart painted with Bronze.

Alas, Poor Yorick

BY CHERYL DARROW

SURFACE: Plaster, cloth

Cheryl found this plaster skull with such a comical grin that she immediately thought it would look great with an aged effect. She also added a whimsical crown.

YOU'LL NEED: A skull figurine, paintbrush, pointed paintbrush, VerDay all-purpose cloth, scissors, stapler, reactive metal paints, and patina solution.

FOR THE SKULL: Paint the entire piece with Iron. Let it dry. Apply more Iron paint to the surface. Spray it with patina solution. Let it dry. Repeat until you are satisfied with the result.

FOR THE CROWN: Cut an 8" x 30" (20.5 x 76cm) crown shape from VerDay all-purpose cloth. Paint the crown with Bronze. Let it dry. Use a pointed brush to paint letters on the crown with Iron. Spray it with patina solution. Let it dry. Overlap and join the ends of the crown using staples. Trim off any excess cloth.

Personalized Words or Initials

BY CHERYL DARROW

SURFACE: Wood or papier-mâché

Everyone likes to see his or her initials, name, or title incorporated in a piece of art. Highlight yours in big wood letters sparkling with reactive metal paint and patina effects.

YOU'LL NEED: 8" (20.5cm)-tall papier-mâché or wood letters, paintbrush, sea sponge, reactive metal paints, and patina solution.

INSTRUCTIONS: Paint the letters with assorted colors of reactive metal paint. Let the paint dry. Sponge more paint in random areas as desired. Spray on patina solution. Let it dry. Repeat until you achieve the look you want.

Flaming Heart Wall Décor

BY CHERYL DARROW

SURFACE: Canvas, metal sheeting, fiberboard

Signify love and emotion by creating a heart icon in the center of a square. Layer the heart and use multiple paint colors to create different shades of rust and verdigris.

YOU'LL NEED: A 12" x 12" (30.5 x 30.5cm) canvas or board with a 6" x 6" (15 x 15cm) recess in the center, a 3½" x 5" (9 x 12.5cm) fiberboard flame, a 2¾" x 3¾" (7 x 9.5cm) scallop-edge fiberboard heart, a 2¼" (5.5cm) fiberboard heart, a 1" (1.5cm) square of black metal sheeting, Mod Podge dimensional glue, sanding block, pointed embossing tool, black acrylic paint, paintbrush, reactive metal paints, and patina solution.

FOR THE HEART'S CENTER SQUARE: Emboss the black metal sheeting with a design of your choice. Cheryl added a border and the word love. Sand the black finish off to reveal the embossed patterns. See page 52 for additional information on embossing.

FOR THE HEART CENTERPIECE: Paint each fiberboard piece with a different color of reactive metal paint. Cheryl used Copper for the flames, Iron for the scalloped-edge heart, and Bronze for the small heart. Allow each piece to dry. Spray them with patina solution. Allow the solution to dry and the paint to change color. Paint the small heart with a thin layer of Mod Podge dimensional glue and let it dry. As it dries, the Bronze will turn a pretty blue color and the paint will crackle. Apply another thin layer of glue to seal the crackled paint. Allow it to dry. Glue the fiberboard pieces together. Use clamps to keep the layers tight until dry.

FOR THE FRAME: Paint the canvas or board with reactive metal paint. Spray it with patina solution. Let it dry. Paint the recessed area black. Glue the embossed metal sheeting to the center of the top heart. Then, glue the heart assembly in the center of the recessed area.

Wood Cross

BY CHERYL DARROW

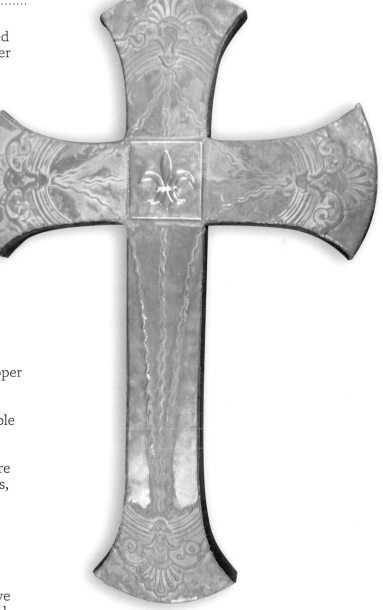

SURFACE: Wood, copper sheeting

Any wood cross can look fabulous with embossed copper sheeting added to the surface. Pure copper or pure brass sheeting can be embossed, and the patina solution will create a verdigris color change on the surface.

YOU'LL NEED: A 14" x 18" (35.5 x 45.5cm) wood cross, pure copper sheeting, steel wool, sanding block, texture plate, embossing machine, a sheet of extra-strength double-sided adhesive (I recommend any brand with a pink color. There are many double-sided adhesive products on the market, and all claim to be strong. Ones with a pink color, though, are by far the strongest.), pointed embossing tool, metal scissors, craft glue (I recommend Elmer's Glue-All, clear spray sealer, reactive metal paint, and patina solution.

INSTRUCTIONS: Paint the wood cross with Copper metal paint. Allow it to dry.

Cover the back of the copper sheeting with a sheet of the adhesive. Lay the sheeting on a table adhesive side down. Place the cross on top of it. Use a pointed tool to trace around the cross. Cut out each arm of the cross separately. When you're finished, you will have the four arms of the cross, plus a square that fits in the center.

Rub the surface of the metal sheeting with steel wool to remove any oil and to shine the surface. Then, emboss the metal sheeting using an embossing machine and texture plate. See page 52 for more detailed information.

Peel the protective backing off of the adhesive attached to the metal sheeting. Adhere the metal sheeting to the corresponding areas of the wood cross. Spray patina solution on the embossed metal. Allow it to dry overnight to change the color. Repeat as desired. Using a piece of steel wool or a sanding block, rub the surface of the metal to polish the raised images. Be sure to seal the finished piece with clear spray sealer or the metal will continue to age.

Birdhouse

BY CHERYL DARROW

SURFACE: Wood

It's just sweet. This cute little birdhouse began as a plain store-bought piece. Reactive metal paints and patina effects brought it to life with rustic elegance.

YOU'LL NEED: A premade wood birdhouse, paintbrush, reactive metal paints, and patina solution.

INSTRUCTIONS: Paint the main body of the birdhouse with Iron. Paint the roof with Copper. While the paint is still wet, spray it with patina solution. Let it dry.

Antique Sugar Mold

SURFACE: Wood

Rescue something old. Preserve both the wood and the nostalgic quality of the piece with a fresh coat of reactive metal paint and patina solution.

YOU'LL NEED: An old wooden sugar mold, paintbrush, reactive metal paints, and patina solution.

INSTRUCTIONS: Paint the sugar mold with Iron. Add drips or streaks to the sides with Brass. While the Brass paint is still wet, brush patina solution along the top edges of the sugar mold and let it drip down the sides. Spray everything with patina solution. Let it dry. Repeat until you achieve the look you want.

Shadowbox

BY KAREN WELLS

SURFACE: Wood

Everything old is old again—but with a fresh appearance. Take an old shadow box, apply reactive metal paint and patina solution, and *voilà*! It's wonderful.

YOU'LL NEED: A wood shadowbox, accessories, paintbrush, sandpaper, spray-on sealer, reactive metal paints, and patina solution.

INSTRUCTIONS: Before you begin, scuff up the shadowbox with sandpaper. Paint it with reactive metal paints. While the paint is wet, spray it with patina solution. Let it dry. Apply the spray-on sealer. Add metal feet and decorative elements inside the box as desired.

Numbered Drawer Set

BY CHERYL DARROW

SURFACE: Wood

This project began as a purchased wood chest and precut wood numbers.

YOU'LL NEED: A wood chest, precut wooden numbers, glue (I recommend Elmer's Glue-All), paintbrush, black acrylic paint, reactive metal paints, and patina solution.

INSTRUCTIONS: Before you begin, paint the chest and numbers black. Let them dry.

You can use a variety of techniques to decorate the numbers. Try covering some with embossed copper metal sheeting and others with embossed VerDay cloth. Just have fun. Experiment by painting some numbers with the reactive metal paints and patina solution. Add textures with bubble wrap, dots, lines, and different brush strokes. While the paint is wet, spray it with patina solution. Let it dry. Adhere the numbers to the chest with wood glue.

Reactive metals paints allow you to create countless projects that all have their own unique look. At the top of this photo is the Shadowbox project, which has a light, bright look. At the bottom is the Numbered Drawer Set, which has a darker, aged look.

Frame Collection

Frames for photos and artwork come in all sizes and styles. These flat frames are perfect for painting and adding texture to create the look of metal and patina.

Bubbles Frame

BY CHERYL DARROW

SURFACE: Wood

Create a unique and personal frame. Add wonderful textures with bubble wrap, a sponge, and stamps.

YOU'LL NEED: A 12" (30.5cm)-square wood frame, Mod Podge matte, paintbrush, bubble wrap, sea sponge, reactive metal paints, and patina solution.

INSTRUCTIONS: Paint the frame with Brass metal paint. Let it dry. Apply Iron paint to bubble wrap and stamp the texture onto the frame. Use a sea sponge to add Bronze in some areas. Spray the frame with patina solution. Let it dry. Repeat until you achieve the look you want. Seal the frame with Mod Podge matte.

Plastic Wrap Texture Frame

BY CHERYL DARROW

SURFACE: Wood

Make your own designer frame using the inexpensive and easy technique of creating texture with crumpled plastic wrap.

YOU'LL NEED: A 12" (30.5cm)-square wood frame, plastic wrap, Mod Podge matte, paintbrush, sea sponge, reactive metal paints, and patina solution.

INSTRUCTIONS: Paint frame with splotches of Bronze and Iron. Let it dry. Use a sea sponge to add Brass and Iron to some areas. Spray the frame with patina solution. Scrunch up some plastic wrap and place a layer of it on top of the frame. Let it dry overnight. Seal the frame with Mod Podge matte.

Vine Frame with Metal

BY ELITIA HART

SURFACE: Wood

Layers of texture and color attract both the eye and the hand to this vibrant frame, which is embellished with a metal vine.

YOU'LL NEED: A 12" (30.5cm)-square wood frame, thin metal sheeting colored green on one side, vine texture plate, texture tool, scissors for metal, sheet of extra-strength double-sided adhesive (I recommend any brand with a pink color. There are many double-sided adhesive products on the market, and all claim to be strong. Ones with a pink color, though, are by far the strongest.), primer, molding paste, clear spray sealer, paintbrush, sea sponge, reactive metal paints, and patina solution.

FOR THE FRAME: Apply splotches of Brass and Iron. Allow it to dry. Use a sea sponge to apply more Brass paint to some areas of the frame. Let it dry.

FOR THE METAL VINES: Place a piece of metal sheeting, green side up, over the vine texture plate. Rub the texture tool over the sheeting on the texture plate to emboss the metal with the vine designs. Fill the backs of the vine leaves with molding paste. Allow it to dry. Attach the double-sided adhesive to the back of the embossed metal. Carefully cut out the vine shapes. Peel the backing from the adhesive on the back of the metal vines, and adhere the vines to the frame.

TO FINISH: Spray the frame and vines with patina solution. Allow it to dry overnight and the paint to change color. Repeat until you get the desired effect. Be sure to seal the finished piece with clear spray sealer or the metal will continue to age.

Copper Frame

BY CHERYL DARROW

SURFACE: Copper sheeting

Add embossed metal to the surface of a frame for an upscale look.

YOU'LL NEED: A 12" (30.5cm)-square wood frame, a 14" (35.5cm)-square piece of pure copper sheeting, steel wool, sanding block, foam brush, pointed embossing tool, various texture plates, sheet of extra-strength double-sided adhesive (I recommend any brand with a pink color. There are many double-sided adhesive products on the market, and all claim to be strong. Ones with a pink color, though, are by far the strongest.), craft knife, paper stump, clear spray sealer, and patina solution.

INSTRUCTIONS: Clean the surface of the copper sheeting by rubbing it with steel wool. Place the sheeting over a texture plate. Rub the embossing tool over the sheeting on the texture plate to emboss the copper with the designs. Add additional embossed textures to other areas of the sheeting as desired.

Apply a sheet of adhesive to the back of the embossed copper. Center the embossed copper over the front of the frame. Use a craft knife to trim the copper so that it extends 1" (2.5cm) beyond all sides of the frame. Cut an opening in the center of the copper to match the opening in the frame, again cutting it to extend 1" (2.5cm) beyond all sides of the frame's opening. Cut diagonal ½" (1.5cm) slits in each corner of the copper. Cut the slits in both the outer corners and the corners for the center opening. Using the paper stump, gently wrap the copper sheeting around the outside and inside edges of the frame. Cut the corner slits a bit longer if needed, and overlap the copper as necessary on the inside corners.

Apply patina solution to the frame with a foam brush. Let it dry. Repeat until you achieve the look you want. Rub the surface of the copper with a sanding block to reveal the embossed shapes. Be sure to seal the finished piece with clear spray sealer or the metal will continue to age.

Embossed Metal Sheeting

SURFACE: Metal sheeting, canvas

Pure metal sheeting is available in rolls and in sheets. It can easily be cut to size with scissors designed for metal. Metal sheeting also comes in several thicknesses. Lightweight metal sheeting in pure copper or pure brass is recommended. (Note: Only pure metal can be altered with patina solution.) You can emboss these sheets using a texture plate and texture tool, or by passing the metal and texture plate through an embossing machine, like the Big Shot.

YOU'LL NEED: An 8" x 8" (20.5 x 20.5cm) canvas panel, a 6" x 6" (15 x 15cm) piece of pure copper sheeting, a 5" x 5" (12.5 x 12.5cm) piece of chipboard, steel wool, sanding block, texture plate, embossing machine, sheet of extra-strength double-sided adhesive (I recommend any brand with a pink color. There are many double-sided adhesive products on the market, and all claim to be strong. Ones with a pink color, though, are by far the strongest.), foam brush, clear spray sealer, glue, reactive metal paints, and patina solution.

BEFORE YOU BEGIN: Paint the canvas with Iron. Spray it with patina solution. Allow it to dry overnight. Rub the surface of the copper sheeting with steel wool to remove any oil and to shine the surface.

1 Emboss the copper sheeting with the desired texture. An embossing machine, such as the Big Shot, will make this process very easy. First, place a carrier and your desired texture plate in the embossing machine.

2 Position the copper sheeting on top of the plate.

3 Cover the metal with layers of padding. Refer to the manufacturer's instructions for layering.

4 Pass the metal sheeting and texture plate through the machine by turning the handle. This transfers the images on the texture plate to the metal.

5 Apply patina solution to the embossed copper with a foam brush. Allow it to dry overnight to change color.

6 Using a piece of steel wool or a sanding block, rub the copper's surface to polish the raised images.

WHEN FINISHED: Secure the chipboard to the center of the canvas with glue. Let it dry. Apply a sheet of adhesive to the back of the embossed copper. Remove the backing from the adhesive and adhere the embossed copper to the center of the chipboard. Be sure to seal the finished piece with clear spray sealer or the metal will continue to age.

Display for Rust and Patina Art

BY CHERYL DARROW

Cheryl loves her collection of small projects colored with reactive metal paints and patina solution. The pieces you create will be your personal collection. The images and embellishments will reflect your style and taste. What's important is to gather up these things and display them. This project will give you a way to do so.

YOU'LL NEED: A 12" x 12" (30.5 x 30.5cm) board with a cradle frame, a 12" x 12" (30.5 x 30.5cm) piece of black felt, hook-and-loop tape with sticky backing, all-purpose glue (I recommend Elmer's Glue-All), paintbrush, black acrylic paint, small rust and patina items.

INSTRUCTIONS: Paint the board black. Allow it to dry. Glue the felt to the front of the board. Let the glue dry. Adhere small rust and patina items to the felt using the hook-and-loop tape. Change out the items whenever you desire.

Woven Basket

BY SUZANNE MCNEILL

SURFACE: Wood

We all need containers. Baskets are handy places to drop the mail, store napkins, toss papers to be sorted later, and tote your craft supplies from place to place.

YOU'LL NEED: A woven wood basket (one with wide slats is best), paintbrush, reactive metal paints, and patina solution.

INSTRUCTIONS: Paint the basket with Copper. Spray it with patina solution. Allow it to dry. Brush Iron onto the vertical slats and around the top rim of the basket. Spray it with patina solution. Allow it to dry.

Woven Paper Art

BY SUZANNE MCNEILL

SURFACE: Paper, stretched canvas

Dress up simple canvas hangings or other projects with woven strips of paper. Add reactive metal paint and patina solution to create the upscale look of woven strips of metal.

YOU'LL NEED: A 12" x 12" (30.5 x 30.5cm) stretched canvas, an 8" x 8" (20.5 x 20.5cm) canvas panel (for Woven Diamond), a 6" x 6" (15 x 15cm) canvas panel (for Woven Diamond), 140# watercolor paper, all-purpose glue (I recommend Elmer's Glue-All), bristle paintbrush, wax paper, sludge, reactive metal paints, and patina solution.

Weaving paper strips

This is a simple process. A bit of waiting is involved to allow the corners and edges to adhere before weaving the next strip. Note: In the directions, I refer to vertical (dark) strips and horizontal (light) strips.

1 Tear twelve equally sized strips from the watercolor paper. Paint the strips with reactive metal paint. Allow them to dry.

2 Use glue to attach one vertical strip and one horizontal strip at a 90-degree angle. Hold or clamp the strips together at one corner until they are dry (about 5 to 20 minutes).

3 Use glue to attach the five remaining dark vertical strips to the light horizontal strip you glued in Step 2. Be sure to alternate the position of the dark vertical strips, gluing one on top of the horizontal strip, the next one underneath, and so on. Hold or clamp the strips together until dry.

4 Weave a light horizontal strip between the vertical strips, positioning it next to the first horizontal strip. Alternate the weave you use for the horizontal strips, starting out weaving over/under, and then the next row under/over, and so on.

5 Weave the remaining light horizontal strips into the dark vertical strips, alternating the weave pattern for each horizontal strip.

6 Adjust the strips as necessary until they are all centered. Add a dab of glue under each loose end. Clamp the strips together until they are dry. Once your paper strips are woven together, you can attach them to canvas art or other projects.

WOVEN SQUARE: Paint the 12" x 12" (30.5 x 30.5cm) stretched canvas with Iron. Spray it with patina solution and allow it to dry. Create a woven square using twelve 1¼" x 7½" (3 x 19cm) torn strips of watercolor paper. Paint six of the strips with Iron metal paint and the remaining six with sludge. Spray patina solution over everything. Allow it to dry overnight. Add more paint and patina solution in areas as desired. Glue the woven square in the center of the canvas. Place wax paper over the entire project and place a book or heavy object on top so everything dries flat. Allow it to dry.

WOVEN DIAMOND: Paint the 12" x 12" (30.5 x 30.5cm) stretched canvas with Bronze, the 8" x 8" (20.5 x 20.5cm) canvas panel with Iron, and the 6" x 6" (15 x 15cm) canvas panel with Brass. Spray the canvases with patina solution and allow them to dry. Create a woven square using twelve 1" x 6" (2.5 x 15cm) torn strips of watercolor paper. Paint six of the strips with Iron metal paint and the remaining six with sludge. Spray patina solution over everything. Allow it to dry overnight. Glue the 8" x 8" (20.5 x 20.5cm) canvas panel to the center of the 12" x 12" (30.5 x 30.5cm) canvas. Glue the 6" x 6" (15 x 15cm) canvas panel on point in the center of the 8" x 8" (20.5 x 20.5cm) canvas panel. Glue the woven square on top. Place wax paper over the entire project and place a book or heavy object on top so all the layers dry flat together. Allow it to dry. Add more paint and patina solution in areas as desired.

Natural Gourds

BY SUZANNE MCNEILL

SURFACE: Gourds, clay

Gourds are nature's gift to every artist. If you have never worked with a gourd before, I encourage you to try it. It's addictive. Every gourd has its own personality and shape. Like wood, gourds readily accept reactive metal paints and patina solution, making them easy to work with for rust and patina style projects. I have used gourds as my canvas for years, drawing on them, painting them, carving them, and stamping them. I was so excited to try this new metallic technique on them. I love the effects these paints produce on the gourds.

YOU'LL NEED: A gourd, face mold, epoxy resin clay (such as Apoxie Clay), disposable gloves, spray release agent (or nonstick cooking spray), rubbing alcohol, pointed tool, metal scrub brush, glue, paintbrush, sea sponge, soft cloth, reactive metal paints, and patina solution.

1 Soak a natural gourd in a bowl of water (place a wet towel on top of the gourd) for about 30 minutes to soften any dried residue on the surface. Rub it with a metal scrubber until clean. Allow the gourd to dry overnight. If you'd like to skip this step, clean gourds can be purchased from *welburngourdfarm.com* and from *wuertzfarm.com*.

2 Prepare the mold by spraying the inside with a thin coat of spray release agent or nonstick cooking spray. Open your containers of clay.

3 If you are using a dual-agent clay, knead equal amounts of the clay mediums together until they are thoroughly mixed. Be sure to refer to the manufacturer's instructions for the type of clay you are using. Press a small chunk of clay into the face mold until the clay is level with the back of the mold. It is helpful to wear disposable gloves when working with clay.

4 Wait 30 minutes to 1 hour to let the clay "set up" in the mold. Before the clay starts to get hard, carefully flex the mold and gently remove the clay face. Position the face on the gourd. Most epoxy resin clays will adhere firmly to the surface. If the face does not adhere to the gourd after it hardens, reinforce the bond with glue. Allow it to dry overnight. Shape the clay face to the curve of the gourd. Alter the face's expression or appearance a bit if desired. For example, you could pinch a narrower chin, or create wider cheeks. You can also use a pointed tool to add detail.

5 Depending on the room temperature, the clay face will begin to harden after about 3 hours and will be totally hard in 5 to 6 hours. Use a soft cloth and rubbing alcohol to gently clean the spray release and any additional oil or residue off of the face. Be sure to clean down in the crevices, because paints won't adhere to any spray release residue. Repeat Steps 2–5 to create and attach as many additional faces as desired.

6 Use a brush to apply reactive metal paints to the gourd and to the faces. Most of the gourds shown were painted with Iron, and the faces were painted with Brass, Bronze, or Copper. The large bowl was painted with Copper and the faces with Iron.

7 Use a sea sponge or brush to apply more reactive metal paint to any desired areas. Spray the surface with patina solution.

8 Allow the color to change and the solution to dry overnight.

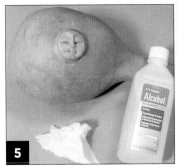

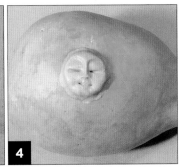

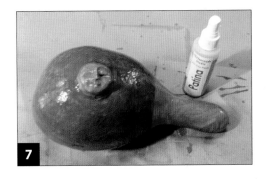

Treasures Unearthed: Metal Jewelry

BY SUZANNE MCNEILL

SURFACE: Metal, wood, papier-mâché, clay

Pendants and jewelry can be made from a wonderful array of found objects because they look rich after you apply the reactive metal paints and patina solution. Items like clay, safety pins, washers, decorative beads, metal charms, and even pieces of antique jewelry can be combined and restored to useful beauty. The process is simple: paint, patina, and seal. Then string your items into something fabulous.

Using found metal

Working with various metal pieces for jewelry is an experimental process. Test the patina solution on a variety of metal objects. Try applying it directly to can lids, drink cans, old bottle caps, pure copper or brass sheeting, safety pins, pure copper or iron wire,

metal washers, or any other pieces of found metal you have. Select the pieces that react with the patina solution in a way you like and use these for your jewelry creations. Remember to check parking lots or the street for found metal items that you can use. Some of these might already have started to develop natural rust and patina.

Once you've made your selection, prepare the surface of the items by cleaning them thoroughly. Scuff off any shiny lacquers or finishes that would prevent the patina solution from reacting with the metal.

Once your jewelry piece is complete, be sure to seal it. Spraying it with a clear sealer is the easiest way to do this. Spray one side of your jewelry piece and allow it to dry. Turn the piece over, spray the other side, and allow it to dry.

DECORATIVE CHARMS: Pure copper, iron, and brass charms will react with patina solution. Clean the surface of the charms with steel wool. Simply spray your desired charms with patina solution and allow them to dry. Note: Many inexpensive charms might be made to look like metal, but have actually been anodized, coated with lacquer, or given a metal finish. Be sure to use charms that are made of pure metal.

SAFETY PINS: Safety pins can be strung on a necklace as charms. Safety pins are an inexpensive staple for sewers and crafters. Purchase the most inexpensive ones you can find. Although they have a metallic coating, this will quickly dissolve under the patina solution, and you will be left with a wonderful rusty surface. Spray the pins with patina solution and allow them to dry.

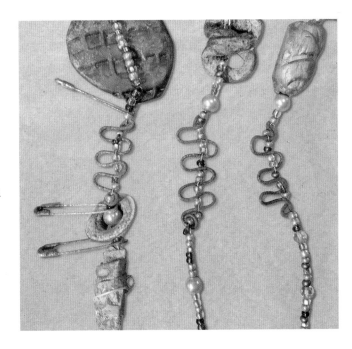

WIRE: Wrap and bend wire into interesting shapes to create beads, links, or other jewelry elements. Use thick wire (12- or 16-gauge) for bent pieces that need to hold their shape. Use wire with a medium thickness (18- or 20-gauge) to wrap beads and to make more intricate shapes. Spray patina solution on your wire creations and allow them to dry. Note: Many inexpensive wires might be made to look like metal, but have actually been anodized, coated with lacquer, or given a metal finish. Be sure to use pure metal wire.

WRAPPED COPPER BEADS: When pure copper sheeting reacts with patina solution, it turns a beautiful green color. You can use wrapped copper sheeting to create a collection of patina copper beads. Use scissors for metal to trim the copper sheeting into long triangular strips. Be careful when cutting the metal because the edges can be sharp. Fold the long edges of the strips under ⅛" (0.5cm) to eliminate sharp edges. Beginning with the wide end, roll each triangular strip around a dowel stick. Hold the metal sheeting in position and secure its shape by wrapping it with pure metal wire. Remove the dowel. Spray the wrapped beads with patina solution and allow them to dry.

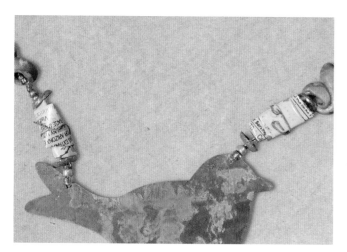

DRINK CAN BEADS: Cut both ends off of a metal drink can with a craft knife. Be careful when cutting the can because the edges can be very sharp. Gently flatten the body of the can. Use scissors for metal to cut the flattened can into long triangular strips. Fold the long edges of the strips under ⅛" (0.5cm) to eliminate sharp edges. Beginning with the wide end, roll each triangular strip around a dowel stick. Hold the metal in position and secure its shape by wrapping it with pure metal wire. Remove the dowel. Spray the beads with patina solution and allow them to dry.

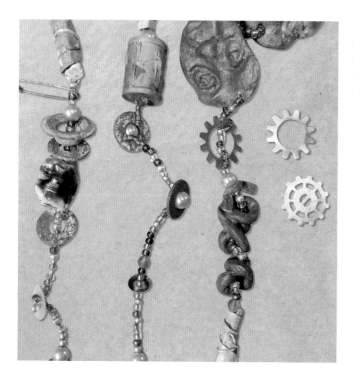

METAL WASHERS: Washers are available in many sizes and decorative shapes. Most washers are made from iron or steel, so they will react with the patina solution nicely. Spray the washers with patina solution and allow them to dry.

WOOD OR PAPIER-MÂCHÉ MEDALLIONS:

Choose a precut wood or papier-mâché piece about 3" to 4" (7.5 to 10cm) in size. Drill two small holes near the top for stringing. Use different techniques to create texture and patina effects. For the wood bird, I squeezed lines of Elmer's Glue-All onto the surface. Once the glue dried, I painted over the surface with the reactive metal paint. For the papier-mâché star, I painted each section with a different reactive metal paint. Spray your painted items with patina solution and allow them to dry.

WOOD BEADS AND SPOOLS: Suspend wood beads or spools on a piece of sturdy wire to hold them in place. Paint each bead with reactive metal paint. Spray them with patina solution and allow them to dry.

MOLDED CLAY BEADS: If you are using a dual-agent epoxy resin clay, knead equal amounts of the clay mediums together until they are thoroughly mixed. Be sure to follow the manufacturer's instructions for the brand of clay you are using. It's helpful to wear disposable gloves when working with clay. Let the clay sit for about 30 minutes. Before the clay starts to get hard, press small pieces into the desired bead shapes. If desired, add stamped designs or textures to the clay. Alternately, form the beads using molds to create unique shapes or faces. Use a pointed tool like an awl to carefully punch one or two holes through the beads for stringing. Put the beads on wax paper to harden. Depending on the room temperature, the clay will harden after about 3 hours and will be totally hard in 5 to 6 hours. Use a brush to apply reactive metal paints to the hardened clay beads. Spray them with patina solution and allow them to dry.

Stringing a necklace

Once you have created your collection of rust and patina charms, dangles, or beads, it's time to use them to create a piece of jewelry.

YOU'LL NEED: Crimp beads, beading wire, clasp, crimp pliers, rust and patina charms, dangles, or beads, and additional beads as desired.

INSTRUCTIONS: To begin, string a crimp bead onto a length of beading wire. Then, string on one end of the clasp. Bring the end of the wire back through the crimp bead, and slide the crimp bead against the clasp. Use the crimp pliers to crimp the bead so it will stay in place on the wire.

String your rust and patina beads and any additional beads onto the wire until your piece reaches the desired length.

To add some extra flair with dangles, string 1" to 2" (2.5 to 5cm) of beads onto the wire, then string on a washer, charm, or large bead. Skipping the end bead or charm, bring the end of the wire back through the beads. This will create dangles on your piece of jewelry. Add as many dangles as desired, stringing as many beads between each one as you want.

When you have strung all the beads you want, string a crimp bead and the other end of the clasp onto the wire. Bring the end of the wire back through the crimp bead and slide it against the clasp. Use the pliers to crimp the bead in place.

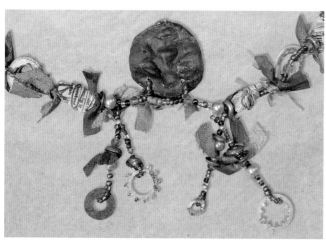

You can add bead dangles at any point along your necklace for a special touch. You can also tie strips of colored silk fabric or ribbon to the necklace to add bright color.

Dancing Queen Doll

BY CHERYL DARROW

SURFACE: Fiberboard, metal sheeting

She is the star of any décor. Embellish her with a puffy tulle skirt and ribbon.

YOU'LL NEED: Precut fiberboard pieces for a 16" (40.5cm)-tall doll, embossed metal for the center of the face, a 4" (10cm)-diameter metal circle to frame the face, two 8" x 36" (20.5 x 91.5cm) pieces of black tulle fabric, 4 large buttons, 24" (61cm) of wire, all-purpose craft glue (I recommend Elmer's Glue-All), 1" (2.5cm)-wide silk ribbon, needle, pliers, strong thread, paintbrush, reactive metal paints, and patina solution.

INSTRUCTIONS: Brush large patches of Bronze on the fiberboard body, arms, and legs, and then add small patches of Iron. Spray the fiberboard with the patina solution and allow it to dry. Turn the body, arms, and legs over. Repeat the application of reactive metal paints and patina solution as desired. Allow it to dry.

Cut a 3" (7.5cm)-diameter circle from embossed metal (see page 52 for embossing instructions). Place the 3" (7.5cm) circle inside of the 4" (10cm) metal circle. Use pliers to bend up the edges of the 4" metal circle to form a cup shape around the small circle. Glue the small circle to the large circle, and glue the large circle to the body.

Take a 6" (15cm) length of wire and thread it, from back to front, through the body, an arm, and then a button. Then thread the end back through the layers. Twist the ends to secure the wire. Cut off any excess wire. Repeat with the remaining arm and each leg.

Layer the pieces of tulle on top of one another. Use a needle and thread to sew a running stitch

through both layers along one of the long edges, stitching 1" (2.5cm) away from the edge. Gently pull one end of the thread to gather the tulle. Wrap it around the doll's body and tie a knot with the thread to secure it. Wrap the ribbon around the doll's waist and secure it with a bow.

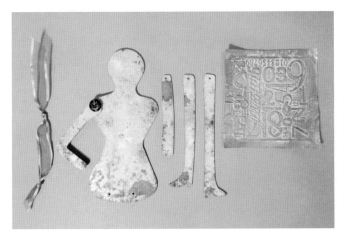

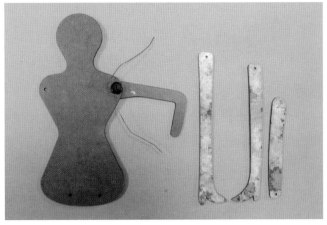

Wild Animals Necklace

Create exotic, gallery-quality jewelry using inexpensive supplies. This necklace was made from plastic toy animals, bits of wire, and leftover beads.

YOU'LL NEED: Small plastic toy animals, assorted beads, pure copper wire, sandpaper, braided leather necklace, paintbrush, wax paper, reactive metal paints, and patina solution.

INSTRUCTIONS: Scuff the surface of the plastic toy animals by rubbing them with sandpaper. Paint one side of the animals with Iron metal paint and set them on wax paper to dry. Spray them with patina solution, and allow them to dry. Turn the animals over and paint the other side. Spray them with patina solution. Allow them to dry. Wrap the animals with the copper wire, adding beads to the wire as desired.

String 1" to 2" (2.5 to 5cm) of assorted beads on a piece of beading wire. Skipping the last bead, bring the end of the wire back through the beads to make a dangle. Use the plastic animals for the ends of the dangles as desired. Wrap the ends of the dangles around the braided leather necklace. Secure the wire ends by bringing the wire back through the beads or through the braided leather necklace.

From left to right: Wood Bangle, Button Bangle Bracelet, and two Embellished Bracelets.

Wood Bangle

BY CHERYL DARROW

SURFACE: Wood

Turn a simple wood bangle bracelet into an expensive-looking "metal" bracelet.

YOU'LL NEED: A wood bangle bracelet, Mod Podge matte, sea sponge, reactive metal paints, and patina solution.

INSTRUCTIONS: Sponge the reactive metal paint onto the bangle. Spray it with patina solution. Allow it to dry. Repeat on the other side of the bangle. Seal the bangle with Mod Podge matte.

Button Bangle Bracelet

BY CHERYL DARROW

SURFACE: Cloth

VerDay all-purpose cloth is perfect for jewelry. The cloth takes reactive metal paint and patina solution well and the edges do not fray. For this project, start out by going through your button box. You will probably find one or two huge buttons that have been there since your grandmother gave the box to you. This project gives you an opportunity to bring antique buttons out into the light of day and show them off on a simple, yet attractive, bangle.

YOU'LL NEED: VerDay all-purpose cloth, large button, large two-piece sew-in snap, needle, thread, paintbrush, Mod Podge matte, reactive metal paints, and patina solution.

INSTRUCTIONS: Brush patches of Iron and Bronze metal paint onto the VerDay cloth. Spray the cloth with patina solution. Allow it to dry. Repeat on the opposite side of the cloth. Seal the cloth with Mod Podge matte. Cut a 2" (5cm)-wide strip that is long enough to fit around your wrist, plus 2" (5cm). About 9" (23cm) works well. Fit the cloth around your wrist, overlapping the ends until it fits as you desire. Mark the position of the snap closure on the ends of the strip. Sew each part of the snap in place by hand on the ends of the strip. Cover the snap thread on the outside of the bangle by sewing the large button in place on top of it.

Embellished Bracelets

BY SUZANNE MCNEILL

SURFACE: Cloth

Turn VerDay cloth into a classy bracelet that looks like pricey metal.

YOU'LL NEED: VerDay cloth, double-sided hook-and-loop tape, heavy black thread, large embroidery needle, Mod Podge matte, sea sponge, reactive metal paints, and patina solution.

INSTRUCTIONS: Sponge reactive metal paints onto the VerDay cloth. Spray it with Patina solution. Allow it to dry. Repeat with another color of paint on the reverse side. Seal the cloth with Mod Podge matte. Allow it to dry. Cut a 1¼" (3cm)-wide strip that is long enough to fit around your wrist, plus 2" (5cm). About 9" (23cm) works well. Fit the cloth around your wrist, overlapping the ends until it fits as you desire. Mark the position of the hook-and-loop tape closure on the ends of the strip. Adhere the hook-and-loop tape pieces in place.

From extra VerDay cloth, cut out 5 each: 1" (2.5cm) circles, 1" (2.5cm) squares, and ½" (1.5cm) squares. Position the pieces on the bracelet band as desired. If you want, make multiple bracelet bands and use the shapes across all of them. Sew the shapes in place on the bracelet, tying a knot on the top to secure them. Trim the thread ends to ½" (1.5cm) long.

Embossed Cloth Jewelry Medallions

BY CHERYL DARROW

SURFACE: Cloth

One unique characteristic of VerDay cloth is that it can be embossed. VerDay cloth holds an imprint and makes beautiful designs. Use almost any brand of embossing machine and embossing folders or texture plates to give this cloth an extra-special touch.

A necklace made of torn silk fibers is flouncy and very soft against your skin. The fibers also complement the vintage look of embossed pendants.

Tie knots at intervals along the silk and add beads and embossed pendants between the knots as desired.

YOU'LL NEED: VerDay cloth, two eyelets, strips of torn silk fabric or ribbon, texture plate, embossing machine, ink pad, paintbrush, reactive metal paints, and patina solution.

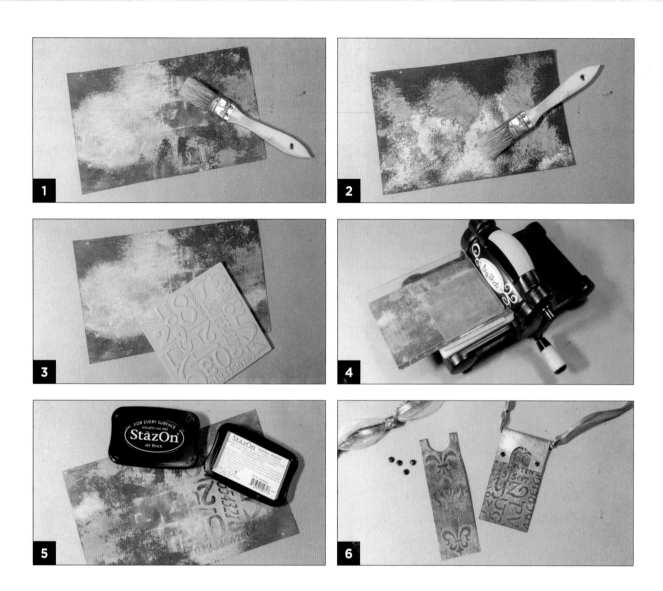

1 Brush patches of Iron and Bronze metal paint onto the VerDay Cloth.

2 Spray the cloth with patina solution. Allow it to dry. Repeat for the reverse side of the cloth.

3 Cut a pendant of the size and shape you want from the cloth. If desired, use the pattern at the right. Place the pendant over the desired texture plate.

4 Cover the pendant with a pad. Run it through an embossing machine.

5 Rub the embossed surface with an inkpad to make the raised images stand out.

6 If using the pendant pattern, fold the rounded end over. Punch two holes through the folded over end on each side. Secure the holes with eyelets. If you are making a pendant with a different shape, punch the holes near the top and secure them with eyelets. Thread the pendant onto your torn silk necklace. Tie knots to secure it as needed.

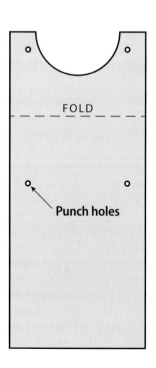

FOLD

Punch holes

Holiday Ornament Collection

During the winter holidays, ornament shapes abound. These give a wonderful opportunity to experiment with reactive metal paints and patina solution while making gifts for all your friends.

Whimsy Ornament

BY CHERYL DARROW

....

SURFACE: Cloth

....

Create a fun spinning ornament with VerDay cloth. Adjust the basic pattern to the size that you want or create your own pattern.

YOU'LL NEED: An 8"x 8" (20.5 x 20.5cm) piece of VerDay cloth, mini brads, ribbon, paintbrush, craft knife, cutting mat, reactive metal paints, and patina solution.

INSTRUCTIONS: Paint one side of the cloth with Iron. Spray it with patina solution. Let it dry. Paint the other side with Bronze. Spray it with patina solution. Let it dry. You can cut any shape you desire from the cloth. If you wish to make the ornament as shown, follow the instructions and diagrams below.

Use a sharp craft knife and a cutting mat to cut slits in the cloth as shown in the diagram below. Fold the edges of the cloth to meet as shown. Secure each overlapping section with a mini brad. Punch a hole in the top of the ornament and tie on a ribbon for a hanger.

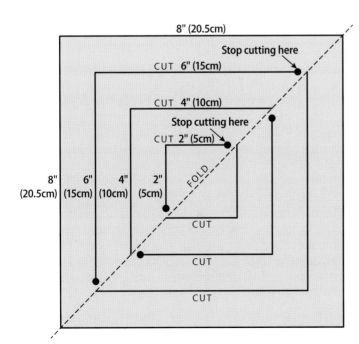

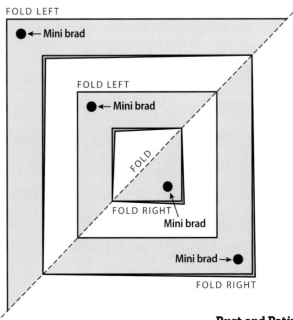

Wood Ornaments

BY CHERYL DARROW

SURFACE: Wood

A sealer with a glossy finish really brings out the sparkle and shine on these fabulous pieces. Hang one in your window or in your car, or wear it as a necklace.

YOU'LL NEED: A 4" to 6" (10 x 15cm) precut wood cross or other shape, Mod Podge dimensional glue, paintbrush, reactive metal paints, and patina solution.

INSTRUCTIONS: Apply reactive metal paint to the wood shape as desired. Spray it with patina solution. Let it dry. Seal the ornament by painting on a very thin coat of Mod Podge dimensional glue. Hang the finished piece from a chain or ribbon.

Cutout Snowflakes

BY SUZANNE MCNEILL

SURFACE: Chipboard, wood, or felt

Whether you use chipboard, wood, or felt, these ornaments are fun to make. Apply a different color of reactive metal paint on each side so the ornament will change as it spins.

YOU'LL NEED: A 9" (23cm)-diameter cutout snowflake, paintbrush, reactive metal paints, and patina solution.

INSTRUCTIONS: Paint one side of the snowflake with Iron. Spray it with patina solution. Let it dry. Paint the other side with Bronze. Spray it with patina solution. Let it dry.

Papier-Mâché Ornaments

BY SUZANNE MCNEILL

SURFACE: Papier-mâché

Be creative when you paint these charming ornaments. Paint sections with different colors and textures.

YOU'LL NEED: Assorted 6" (15cm) papier-mâché shapes, paintbrush, reactive metal paints, and patina solution.

INSTRUCTIONS: Apply reactive metal paints to one side of the papier-mâché shapes as desired. Spray them with patina solution. Let them dry. Paint the other side. Spray them with patina solution. Let them dry.

I painted my heart ornament with Brass. Then, I applied patina solution using bubble wrap. I painted the angel with Iron on the wings and head and Copper on the body. For the Christmas ball, I painted each side with a different color and applied patina solution to each side.

Mixed-Media Booklet

BY CHERYL DARROW

SURFACE: Cloth, paper

What a wonderful and fun little booklet. It is filled with rustic pages altered with images, rust, and patina.

YOU'LL NEED: VerDay cloth, tan cardstock or builder's paper, 1" (2.5cm)-wide blue painter's tape, clippings of words and images, large needle, waxed linen or sturdy twine, paintbrush, Mod Podge matte, reactive metal paints, and patina solution.

INSTRUCTIONS: Create accents for your pages by cutting a 9" x 18" (23 x 45.5cm) piece of VerDay cloth. Tear several strips of blue painter's tape in half lengthwise to make ½" (1.5cm)-wide strips. Lay the VerDay cloth on a piece of builder's paper. Secure the four edges to the paper with the tape. Use the tape to create a grid over the cloth. Place a piece of tape down the vertical centerline and across the horizontal centerline. Add two more vertical strips of tape to create a grid of eight boxes on the cloth as shown below.

Paint alternating colors of reactive metal paint in each square of the grid. Mix colors in some of the squares. Spray the paint with patina solution and allow it to dry.

Adhere clippings of images and words to the squares with Mod Podge matte. Add rubber stamp images and additional accents as desired. Set the accent cloth aside for now.

For the cover, cut a 5½" x 11" (14 x 28cm) piece of VerDay cloth. Apply Iron and Bronze metal paints to the cover. Spray it with patina solution. Let it dry. Turn the cover over and apply reactive metal paints to the other side as desired. Spray it with patina solution, and let it dry.

For the pages, cut six pieces of 4½" x 10" (11.5 x 25.5cm) builder's paper or tan cardstock. Apply Iron and Bronze metal paints to the paper. Totally cover some pages with reactive metal paints. Apply reactive metal paints only to the edges of other pages. Spray patina solution on the pages. Let them dry. Repeat on the other side.

Remove the blue tape grid from the accent cloth you decorated previously. Separate the squares by cutting them apart in the center of the borders left by the tape. Color the blank edges as desired.

Use Mod Podge matte to secure the cloth accent squares to the paper pages as desired. Allow them to dry. Add additional accents, words, and marks as desired.

Fold the cover and each page in half widthwise. Open the fold. Center the pages on top of the inside of the cover, using the fold line to align them. Punch four holes along the fold through all the layers.

Cut a 16" (40.5cm) piece of waxed linen or sturdy twine. Weave it in and out of the holes in the spine of the book, returning to the starting point. Tie a sturdy knot on the inside of the book cover. Cut off excess twine, leaving 1" (2.5cm) tails.

Candy Dish

BY CHERYL DARROW

SURFACE: Cloth

Keep this little container at your desk so your favorite candy is always within reach. This little dish is also handy for storing small supplies like paper clips, rubber bands, or brads.

YOU'LL NEED: VerDay cloth, Mod Podge matte, four brads, paintbrush, reactive metal paints, and patina solution.

INSTRUCTIONS: Cut a 7" x 7" (18 x 18cm) square of VerDay cloth. Paint one side with Iron and spray it with patina solution. Let it dry. Paint the other side with Brass and spray it with patina solution. Let it dry.

Fold up the corners of the cloth to form a bowl shape. Punch a hole through the overlapping folds of cloth at each corner. Put a brad through each hole so the bowl will hold its shape.

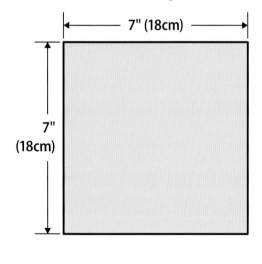

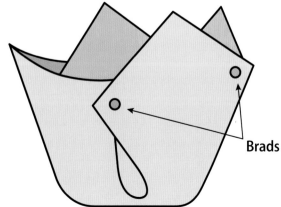

Brads

Wine Tote

BY CHERYL DARROW

SURFACE: Cloth

Perfect for your next dinner party, this classy tote makes an impressive hostess gift.

YOU'LL NEED: VerDay cloth, black acrylic paint, blue painter's tape, sewing machine, black thread, paintbrush, reactive metal paints, and patina solution.

INSTRUCTIONS: Cut four 5" x 13" (12.5 x 33cm) pieces of VerDay cloth for the sides of the tote. Cut one 5" x 5" (12.5 x 12.5cm) piece of cloth for the bottom. Cut one 1½" x 12" (4 x 30.5cm) piece of cloth for the handle. Sew the four side pieces together along the long edges using a ¼" (0.5cm) seam allowance.

Paint the front side of the tote body with black acrylic paint. Add an accent if desired by using the tape to mark off a section across the front of the cloth. Paint between the strips with Iron and Bronze metal paint. Spray the paint with patina solution. Let it dry. Paint the back side of the cloth black. Paint both sides of the bottom and handle black.

Finish the tote by sewing the tote body along the edge to form a tube. Then, sew the bottom and handle pieces in place.

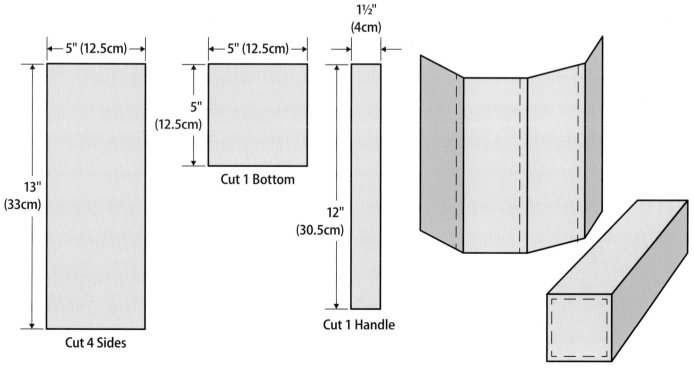

5" (12.5cm)

13" (33cm)

Cut 4 Sides

5" (12.5cm)

5" (12.5cm)

Cut 1 Bottom

1½" (4cm)

12" (30.5cm)

Cut 1 Handle

Cloth Doll

BY SUZANNE MCNEILL

SURFACE: Cloth

Everything about dolls is interesting—especially their importance in art and culture through the ages. Adding to my collection of dolls is always exciting.

YOU'LL NEED: VerDay cloth, a found head from a doll (with hair), all-purpose craft glue (I recommend Elmer's Glue-All), blue painter's tape, paintbrush, wax paper, reactive metal paints, and patina solution.

1 Lay the doll head on a piece of wax paper. Fluff up the hair so that it looks wild and windblown. Drip glue in the hair to hold the wild look in place. Let it dry. Repeat as desired to achieve the effect you desire.

2 Brush and stipple Bronze metal paint randomly over the hair and face. Let it dry.

3 Spray patina solution on the face and hair. Allow the solution to dry overnight and the paint to change color.

4 Use a smaller brush to apply Copper metal paint to the face. Allow it to dry. Apply patina solution if desired or leave the paint color unchanged.

5 Cut a 16" x 24" (40.5 x 61cm) piece of VerDay cloth. Apply Iron metal paint to the cloth. Spray it with patina solution. Let it dry until the color becomes a rusty orange. Apply Copper metal paint to the other side of the cloth. Spray patina solution on the Copper paint. Let it dry until the paint becomes a greenish color.

6 Copy the patterns at the desired size. Cut each piece from the cloth. Glue the heart to the rusty orange side of the apron with the green side of the heart facing out. Let the glue dry.

7 Roll the wedge shape into a cone with the green side facing out. Overlap the ends of the cone about ½" (1.5cm) and glue them in place. Use a piece of painter's tape to hold the ends together until the glue dries.

8 Glue the apron in place over the cone. Glue the doll head at the top of the cone. Allow everything to dry overnight.

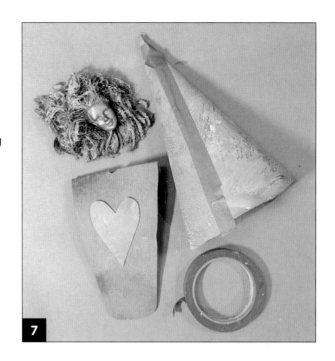

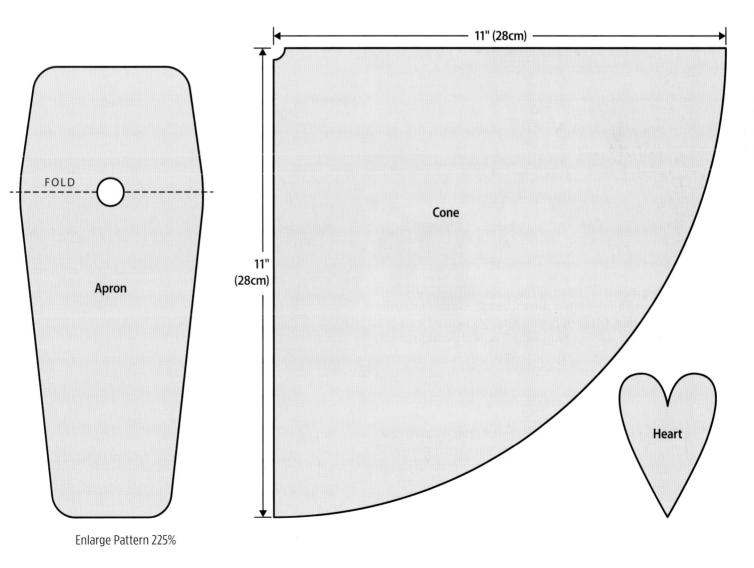

FOLD

Apron

Cone

11" (28cm)

11" (28cm)

Heart

Enlarge Pattern 225%

Vintage Spool Necklace

BY CHERYL DARROW

SURFACE: Wood

Create an eclectic look by combining items that look old.

YOU'LL NEED: A large wood spool, two wood beads, pure copper sheeting, pure copper wire, a sheet of extra-strength double-sided adhesive (I recommend any brand with a pink color. There are many double-sided adhesive products on the market, and all claim to be strong. Ones with a pink color, though, are by far the strongest.), scissors for metal, strips of torn silk fabric or ribbon, steel wool, sanding block, texture tool, texture plate, paintbrush, reactive metal paints, and patina solution.

INSTRUCTIONS: Paint the wood beads and spool with Brass metal paint. Spray them with patina solution and allow them to dry. Cut a strip of copper sheeting to fit around the center of the spool. Rub the surface of the copper with steel wool or a sanding block to shine it. Use a texture tool and texture plate to emboss a design into the copper. Wrap the embossed copper strip around the center of the spool. Secure the ends of the embossed copper strip with the double-sided adhesive.

Thread torn silk fabric or ribbon through the beads and spool, knotting the fabric between each bead. Wrap bits of copper wire around the silk as desired to hold the fabric together and add a bit of sparkle.

Fabric Prints

BY SUZANNE MCNEILL

SURFACE: Fabric

Reactive metal paints and patina solution can be used to create beautiful colors, splashes of texture, and fabulous patterns on fabric to create your own fabric prints. Fabric with reactive metal paints applied should be gently laundered by hand. Don't use any soap.

YOU'LL NEED: Muslin or silk, an item to create texture, builder's paper, freezer paper, paintbrush, reactive metal paints, and patina solution.

INSTRUCTIONS: Cover your work surface with builder's paper and then freezer paper with the shiny side up. Select an item with a shape or texture you would like to transfer to your fabric, such as a foam stamp, the flat side of a plastic crate, or a wood cutout. Paint one side of your chosen item with Iron. Allow the paint to dry completely. Spray patina solution over the Iron paint on your texture item. Immediately, while the patina solution is still wet, place your fabric over the texture item. Press the fabric flat with your hand. Leave the fabric where it is overnight so it absorbs all the color from the texture item. Then, lift the fabric off.

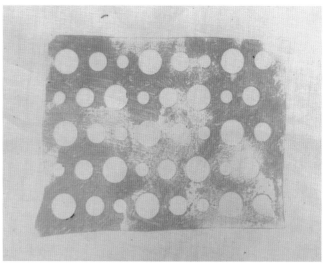

Side of a plastic crate

Foam stamp

Wood cutout

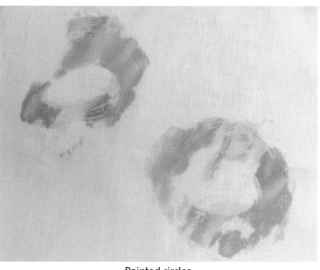

Painted circles

Silk Scarf

BY SUZANNE MCNEILL

SURFACE: Silk

I love experimenting with techniques for embellishing silk scarves. Silk is wonderfully light and it accepts reactive metal paints in interesting ways.

YOU'LL NEED: A silk scarf, builder's paper, freezer paper, a spray bottle with water, paintbrush, reactive metal paints, and patina solution.

INSTRUCTIONS: Cover your work surface with freezer paper (for protection), and then with builder's paper on top. Brush Iron metal paint onto the builder's paper using a pattern of your choice, such as stripes or circles. Allow the paint to dry completely. Paint patina solution over the Iron paint.

Immediately lay a scarf on top of the wet patina solution. Allow it to settle on the paint. Spray the scarf lightly with water from the spray bottle to weigh it down and create more contact with the paint. Let it dry overnight. Iron the scarf to heat-set the color.

If you desire a stronger rust color, paint patina solution on top of the silk scarf after you have put it in place on top of the paint, following the pattern lines you painted previously.

Do not launder your scarf. Remove stains or spots as needed by treating each one gently by hand. Don't use any soap.

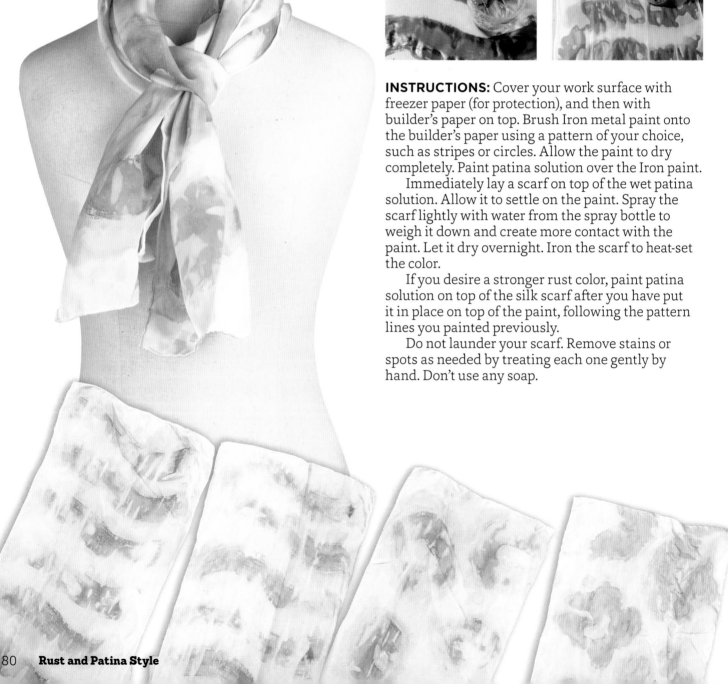

Tote Bag Collection

BY SUZANNE MCNEILL

SURFACE: Canvas

Everyone uses tote bags. Give yours individual pizzazz with reactive metal paints and patina solution.

YOU'LL NEED: A canvas tote bag, blue painter's tape, stencil or large foam stamp of your choice, cardboard, paintbrush, Mod Podge matte, reactive metal paints, and patina solution.

INSTRUCTIONS: Before you begin, iron your bag to remove wrinkles and creases. Place a piece of cardboard inside the bag to protect it from bleed-through. Decorate the outside of the bag as desired using the reactive metal paints and patina solution. Try applying the paint with a stamp or stencil, or use painter's tape to create a fun border.

Use four strips of painter's tape to make a frame in the center of one side of the tote bag. Apply Iron metal paint within the tape frame. Brush small streaks around the outside. Spray patina solution on the bag. Let it dry until the paint changes color.

Apply Bronze metal paint in a square in the center of the Iron section. Allow it to dry. Place a stencil over the center of the Bronze square. Paint the stencil shape on with Iron.

Spray patina solution on the bag. Let it dry until the paint changes color. Remove the painter's tape. Seal the bag with Mod Podge matte.

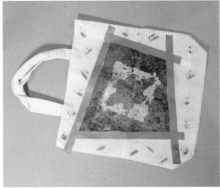

STRIPED TOTE WITH HEART: Apply Iron metal paint to the bag in stripes. Apply Bronze stripes to the bag between the Iron stripes. Spray patina solution on the bag. Let it dry until the paint changes color. Seal the bag with Mod Podge matte. Glue on a heart accent piece (I recommend Goop glue). Let it dry overnight.

DIAMOND TOTE: Use a paintbrush to apply Copper in a diamond shape in the center of the bag. Apply Iron around the outer edges of the bag to create a border. Allow the paint to dry. Use Iron paint to stencil a design in the center of the diamond over the Copper paint. Spray patina solution on the bag. Let it dry until the paint changes color. Seal the bag with Mod Podge matte.

MOTTLED TOTE: Apply Iron metal paint to some areas of the bag. Apply Bronze to the bag in other areas. Spray patina solution on the bag. Let it dry until the paint changes color. Seal the bag with Mod Podge matte.

RECTANGLE TOTE: Use a paintbrush to apply Bronze metal paint around the outer edges of the bag to create a border. Apply Iron to the area inside the Bronze border. Allow it to dry. Apply Bronze paint to a foam stamp. Stamp the design onto the bag. Apply as many additional stamped designs as desired. Spray patina solution on the bag. Let it dry until the paint changes color. Seal the bag with Mod Podge matte.

Rustic Apron

BY CHERYL DARROW

SURFACE: Canvas

Aprons are essential in the art room and in the kitchen. Have fun decorating yours.

YOU'LL NEED: A black canvas apron, blue painter's tape, paintbrush, sea sponge, Mod Podge matte, permanent markers, reactive metal paints, and patina solution.

INSTRUCTIONS: Use strips of painter's tape to create a square in the center of the apron top. Section off any other areas as desired with the tape, like a stripe across the very top of the apron and two diagonal stripes down the front.

Apply Iron metal paint to the center square and any other areas created with the tape. Use a sea sponge to apply Bronze as desired over the Iron paint. Spray patina solution on the apron. Let it dry until the paint changes color. Remove the tape. Seal the apron with Mod Podge matte.

Use a wide black permanent marker to write a word or draw a picture on the center square. Outline the word or design with a gold metallic permanent marker.

This apron has been successfully laundered (no bleach) in a washing machine and dryer. If in doubt, hand wash your project without soap.

Textured Frames

SURFACE: Wood or plastic

Carved and textured surfaces look exceptionally nice with an application of reactive metal paint and patina solution. These inexpensive plastic frames were perfect candidates for embellishment.

YOU'LL NEED: A textured frame, paintbrush, reactive metal paints, and patina solution.

INSTRUCTIONS: Apply reactive metal paint of your desired color to the surface. Spray patina solution on the surface. Let it dry until the paint changes color.

Rust and Patina Journal

BY CHERYL DARROW

SURFACE: Paper, cloth

Sometimes all it takes is a little push in the right direction to discover your hidden talents and abilities. Believe in yourself and your art will take flight.

YOU'LL NEED: VerDay cloth, sewing machine, black thread, printed words on paper, white cardstock, strip of torn muslin fabric, paintbrush, paintbrush to attach to cover, Mod Podge matte, reactive metal paints, and patina solution.

FOR THE COVER: Cut a piece of 9" x 12" (23 x 30.5cm) VerDay cloth. Brush patches of Iron and Bronze metal paint onto the cloth. Spray it with patina solution. Allow it to dry. Repeat for the other side of the cloth, using a different color. Allow it to dry. Zigzag stitch around the edges of the cloth with the sewing machine, adjusting the tension as needed. Adhere words to the cloth

with Mod Podge matte. Position the paintbrush as desired on the cover. Then punch two holes, one on either side of it. Attach the paintbrush to the cloth with a strip of muslin threaded through the punched holes.

FOR THE PAGES: Cut six 8½" x 11" (21.5 x 28cm) pieces of cardstock. Fold each page in half widthwise, and then open them. Layer the pages on top of one another, and then center them on the cloth cover. Sew down the center fold of the pages to secure them to the cover. Tie a strip of muslin around the center fold.

TO FINISH: Embellish the pages by applying reactive metal paints with stencils, stamps, and texture plates as desired. Let the paint dry. Spray it lightly with patina solution and allow everything to dry.

Inspirational Cards or Décor

BY CHERYL DARROW

SURFACE: Paper, chipboard, cloth, or wood

Do you love to play with lettering? Here's your chance. Create paper or wood plaques with meaningful words that sparkle. These hand-painted signs are perfect for your computer desk or workspace—anywhere you need an encouraging word.

RUSTY LETTERING: Cover paper or wood with Iron metal paint. Allow it to dry. Use a soft ¼" or ½" (0.5 or 1.5cm) flat brush to paint on letters and words with patina solution. Allow everything to dry overnight. Repeat the application of the patina solution if desired.

DARK LETTERING: Take a sheet of chipboard that you have already colorized with reactive metal paint and patina solution. Seal it with Mod Podge matte or with clear spray sealer. Let it dry. Use a black marker or calligraphy pen to write words or a saying on the surface.

Canvas Shoes

BY CHERYL DARROW

....

SURFACE: Canvas

....

This art is no accident. Next time you drip paint on your shoes, make it intentional!

YOU'LL NEED: Canvas shoes, duct tape, paintbrush, sea sponge, Mod Podge matte, reactive metal paints, and patina solution.

INSTRUCTIONS: Prepare the shoes by removing the shoelaces. Apply duct tape to the soles to protect them from the paint. Press the tape down well so no paint will get underneath it.

Apply Iron metal paint to the shoes. Use a sea sponge to apply irregular Bronze areas to the shoes. Spray patina solution on the shoes. Let it dry until the paint changes colors. Remove the tape. Seal the shoes with Mod Podge matte.

About Suzanne McNeill

Suzanne McNeill is often known as a trendsetter. Dedicated to hands-on creativity, she constantly tests, experiments, and invents new and exciting things. Artist, designer, TV personality, publisher, workshop instructor, and popular author, Suzanne McNeill has spent a lifetime inspiring and encouraging people of all ages to engage in artistic expression.

Suzanne joined forces with Fox Chapel Publishing in 2011. She continues to share her creativity by authoring books and teaching workshops. Visit Suzanne at *blog.suzannemcneill.com* for events, ideas, activities, and free Zentangle® patterns, or visit *SparksStudioArt.com* to view her personal artwork and descriptions of her classes. Also check out YouTube to view more than 100 video demonstrations from Suzanne on the Zentangle method, quilting, and various other art forms.

Index

NOTE: Page numbers in *italics* indicate projects.

Ideas & Inspirations for Art Journals & Sketchbooks
ISBN 978-1-57421-379-9 **$16.99**
DO3502

Stash & Smash: Art Journal Ideas
ISBN 978-1-57421-409-3 **$16.99**
DO5380

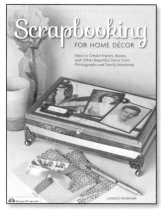

Scrapbooking for Home Décor
ISBN 978-1-57421-411-6 **$19.99**
DO5382

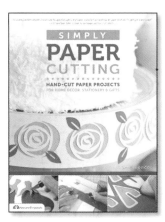

Simply Paper Cutting
ISBN 978-1-57421-418-5 **$19.99**
DO5389

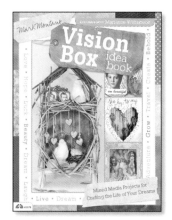

Vision Box Idea Book
ISBN 978-1-57421-407-9 **$16.99**
DO5378

Pulp Fiction, 2nd Edition: Perfect Paper Projects
ISBN 978-1-57421-413-0 **$16.99**
DO5384

Joy of Zentangle®
ISBN 978-1-57421-427-7 **$24.99**
DO5398

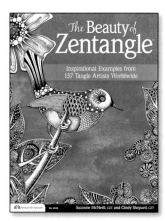

The Beauty of Zentangle®
ISBN 978-1-57421-718-6 **$24.99**
DO5038

The Art of Travel with a Sketchbook
ISBN 978-1-57421-618-9 **$24.99**
DO5308